BUGS
of
NORTHERN CALIFORNIA

John Acorn
Illustrations by Ian Sheldon

LONE
PINE

© 2002 by Lone Pine Publishing
First printed in 2002   10 9 8 7 6 5 4 3 2 1
Printed in Canada

The Publisher: Lone Pine Publishing

1901 Raymond Ave. Suite C	10145 81 Ave.
Renton, WA 98055	Edmonton, AB T6E 1W9
USA	Canada

Website: http://www.lonepinepublishing.com

National Library of Canada Cataloguing in Publication Data
Acorn, John, (date)
   Bugs of Northern California

   Includes bibliographical references and index.
   ISBN 1-55105-320-9

   1. Insects—California, Northern—Identification. 2. Arthropoda—California, Northern—Identification. I. Sheldon, Ian, (date) II. Title.
QL475.C3A26 2001   595.7'09794   C2001-911235-1

Editorial Director: Nancy Foulds
Project Editor: Volker Bodegom
Editorial: Volker Bodegom, Lee Craig
Layout & Production: Arlana Anderson-Hale
Book Design: Robert Weidemann, Heather Markham
Cover Design: Robert Weidemann, Rod Michalchuk
Illustrations: Ian Sheldon
Photography: John Acorn
Separations & Film: Elite Lithographers Co.

Cover illustration: Caterpillar Hunter by Ian Sheldon

The following illustrations are used with the permission of Ian Sheldon © 1999, 2000 & 2001: pp. 28–30; p. 32; pp. 34–38; pp. 40–43; and pp. 45–59.

Many thanks to Great North Productions and photographer Robert van Schaik for the use of the photo on p. 11.

We acknowledge the financial support of the Government of Canada through the Book Publishing Industry Development Program (BPIDP) for our publishing activities.

PC: *04*

CONTENTS

DEDICATION

To the memory of Richard Fall, without whom many of us would never have owned a decent bug net.

ACKNOWLEDGMENTS

As much as I enjoyed writing this book, I enjoyed working with Ian Sheldon even more. I can't thank Ian enough for his dedication to both the art and science of "bugs." As well, this book would not have been possible without the characteristic generosity of many entomologists and arachnologists. In particular, Cheryl Barr reviewed the text and suggested many improvements, and I especially appreciate her Californian perspective on such a Californian book. Felix Sperling, George Ball and Danny Shpeley of the University of Alberta's E.H. Strickland Entomology Museum, as well as Brian Brown and Brian Harris of the Los Angeles County Museum, provided ready access to reference specimens. I would also like to thank the following people for reviewing text and graciously responding to queries: Gary Anweiler, Brian Brown, Rob Cannings, Eric Coombs, Ed Fuller, Robert Holmberg, Rueben Kaufman, Dave Lawrie, James LaBonte, David Maddison, Chris Schmidt, Ales Smetana, Terry Thormin, Richard Westcott, Daryl Williams and Richard Worth. The staff at Lone Pine Publishing have, as usual, been a pleasure to work with, and I would especially like to thank Volker Bodegom, Arlana Anderson-Hale, Lee Craig, Robert Weidemann, Rod Michalchuk, Heather Markham, Nancy Foulds and Shane Kennedy for their contributions. Finally, I would like to thank my wife Dena Stockburger and our sons Jesse and Benjamin for their loving support and for their enthusiasm for my work.

BUTTERFLIES

Western Tiger
Swallowtail, p. 28

Pale Swallowtail
p. 29

Cabbage White
p. 30

Orange & Clouded
Sulphurs, p. 31

California Dogface
p. 32

Spring Azure
p. 33

Purplish Copper
p. 34

Hedgerow
Hairstreak, p. 35

California Dogface
p. 32

Pacific Fritillary
p. 37

Common Buckeye
p. 38

Mourning Cloak
p. 39

California
Tortoiseshell, p. 40

West Coast Lady
p. 41

California Sister
p. 42

Common Ringlet
p. 43

MOTHS

Monarch
p. 44

Polyphemus
Moth, p. 45

California Silk
Moth, p. 46

Hera Buck
Moth, p. 47

MOTHS

Sheep Moth
p. 48

White-lined
Sphinx, p. 49

Big Poplar
Sphinx, p. 50

Tomato Hornworm
Moth, p. 51

Snowberry
Clearwing, p. 52

Edwards'
Glassywing, p. 53

Carpenterworm
Moth, p. 54

California Tent Caterpillar
Moth, p. 55

Yarn Moths
p. 56

Rough Prominent
p. 57

Aholibah
Underwing, p. 58

Darwin's Green
p. 59

Pacific Tiger
Beetle, p. 60

California Tiger
Beetle, p. 61

BEETLES

Long-faced
Carabids, p. 62

Caterpillar Hunter
p. 63

Big Dingy Ground
Beetle, p. 64

Burying Beetles
p. 65

Devil's Coach
Horse, p. 66

May Beetles
p. 67

Ten-lined June
Beetle, p. 68

Rain Beetles
p. 69

BEETLES

Golden Jewel
Beetle, p. 70

Sculptured Pine
Borer, p. 71

Western Eyed Click
Beetle, p. 72

Stink Beetle
p. 73

Ash Gray
Ladybug, p. 74

Convergent
Ladybug, p. 75

California Prionus
p. 76

Ponderous Borer
p. 77

WASPS, BEES & ANTS

Banded Alder
Borer, p. 78

Blue Milkweed
Beetle, p. 79

Stump Stabbers
p. 80

Pacific Cuckoo
Wasp, p. 81

Great Golden
Digger, p. 82

Yellow Jackets
p. 83

Golden Paper
Wasp, p. 84

Cow Killers
p. 85

TWO-WINGED FLIES

Bumble Bees
p. 86

Carpenter Bees
p. 87

Carpenter Ants
p. 88

Giant Crane Flies
p. 89

TWO-WINGED FLIES

Horse Flies
p. 90

Beeish Robber
Flies, p. 91

Sand Dune
Bee Fly, p. 92

Drone Fly
p. 93

ANT LIONS, ETC.

Ant Lions
p. 94

Green Lacewings
p. 95

Snakeflies
p. 96

Big Green
Stink Bugs, p. 97

SUCKING BUGS

Rough Stink
Bugs, p. 98

Harlequin Bug
p. 99

Ambush Bug
p. 100

Western Boxelder
Bug, p. 101

Cicadas
p. 102

Rock Crawlers
p. 103

Road Duster
p. 104

Angular-winged
Katydid, p. 105

GRIGS

Field Crickets
p. 106

Cave Crickets
p. 107

Jerusalem Cricket
p. 108

California Walkingsticks
p. 109

Narrow-winged
Mantid, p. 110

Minor Ground
Mantid, p. 111

California Mantid
p. 112

European Earwig
p. 113

Giant Dampwood
Termites, p. 114

German Cockroach
p. 115

Boreal Bluet
p. 116

Vivid Dancer
p. 117

California Spreadwing
p. 118

Blue-eyed
Darner, p. 119

Green Darner
p. 120

Flame Skimmer
p. 121

Common
Whitetail, p. 122

Variegated
Meadowhawk, p. 123

Stream Skater
p. 124

Giant Water
Bugs, p. 125

Toe Biter
p. 126

Water Boatmen
p. 127

Single-banded
Backswimmer, p. 128

Water Scorpions
p. 129

Whirligig Beetles
p. 130

Giant Diving
Beetles, p. 131

AQUATIC ADULTS

Water Scavenger
Beetle, p. 132

Salmonfly
p. 133

Mayfly Larvae
p. 134

Damselfly Larvae
p. 135

Dragonfly Larvae
p. 136

AQUATIC LARVAE

Caddisfly Larvae
p. 137

Water Tigers
p. 138

Salmonfly Larva
p. 139

Sow Bug
p. 140

NON-INSECT ARTHROPODS

Garden Centipedes
p. 141

Clown Millipede
p. 142

Scorpions
p. 143

Pseudoscorpions
p. 144

Camel Spiders
p. 145

Garden Harvestmen
p. 146

California Ebony
Tarantula, p. 147

Johnson's Jumper
p. 148

Goldenrod Flower
Spider, p. 149

Western Black
Widow, p. 150

Yellow Garden
Spider, p. 151

Long-bodied Cellar
Spider, p. 152

INTRODUCTION

THIS BOOK is for bugsters. If you haven't heard the term, don't feel left out. I think I invented it, with the help of my friends. We needed a word for people who are fascinated by insects and enjoy them for no other reason than their intrinsic niftiness. "Amateur entomologist" seemed too stuffy, as did "insect enthusiast" and "entomophile." "Bugger" is out of the question. So are "bug-nut," and "bug-lover." I did find the term "entomaniac" popular among some of the people I know, but it probably isn't the best one to use as a recruiting tool. Maniacs are crazy, but we bugsters are merely enthusiastic.

Even the word "bug" is fraught with problems. In the strict language of entomology, a bug is a member of the order Hemiptera, often pedantically called "true bugs," although I prefer the more neutral "sucking bugs" myself. The phrase "sucking bugs" refers to their sucking, not chewing, mouthparts. All other insects are simply "insects." In technical language, when one expands the scope to include spiders, centipedes and millipedes, one has to resort to the phrase "terrestrial arthropods." It's tough to say that without sounding pretentious. So let's just cut through all of this confusion and call the critters "bugs," and the people who love them "bugsters." It works for me, and the only reason it was difficult to arrive at is that our language simply hasn't been called upon to develop everyday words to go with these ideas.

The lack of a label for bugsters is odd, given the enduring appeal of bugs. Some, such as butterflies, are beautiful. Others, such as lady-bugs and bumble bees, are familiar personal-ities in the garden. Then there are those that are fascinating in a scary sort of way, such as spiders and scorpions. Finally, there is the wonderful diversity of insect life, and the delight that is generated by such a wide variety of living forms "right under our noses." Biologists these days like to call this wide variety "biodiversity," and there are some biologists who claim that people are naturally predisposed to appreciate and crave contact with it. This idea, in turn, gave rise to the word "biophilia," which can

be translated as "the love of living things." I am not so sure that I agree with the biophilia hypothesis, because there are so many people out there who couldn't care less about the world of plants and animals. For those who feel the connection, however, the idea of biophilia can be a great comfort—it makes us feel normal after all.

Of course, because not all bugs are beneficial to people, and every single one of them is smaller than a hamster, our society as a whole has developed a rather disdainful attitude toward bugs. As a consequence, most of the people who have done things to improve our understanding and appreciation of bugs have been professional biologists. Of these scientists, entomologists study insects, and arachnologists study arachnids. Scientists who study other sorts of bugs are generally called "invertebrate zoologists," and this term can also be used to refer to the whole gang at once.

In northern California, as in other parts of North America, the tradition of bug study has gone on primarily in the universities, as well as in research facilities operated by various levels of government. Forest and crop pests have attracted their share of attention, as have biting flies and other bugs of medical or veterinary importance. Yet some professional bugsters have studied their subjects out of "pure" fascination, and there have also been many talented and devoted amateurs who have contributed to the knowledge of this region's bugs as well.

We seem poised for a resurgence of interest in our arthropod neighbors, what with a proliferation of bug-related movies, children's books and toys in the last few years. I suppose this book will probably be considered part of the same "craze," but I also hope it will survive beyond that. For this reason,

I have tried to make the book as entomologically correct as I could muster, while still retaining a spirit of fun and informality. I've learned, from my participation in the dinosaur craze of the 1980s, that after public attention has passed, we are still left with an interesting subject. As well, the intriguing things about it are still brought forward by the core group of people who cared about it before the fad, and who will continue to care in the future.

There are about 20,000 species of bugs in northern California. This number is a guess, of course, and the reason we don't know exactly is that there are still new species waiting to be discovered by science, and there are many species known elsewhere that are waiting to be found here. Choosing the 125 "coolest" species was a challenge for me. I tried to pick bugs that are either **1) big, 2) colorful, 3) really hard to miss** or **4) extremely weird.**

The point of this book is to introduce you to the bugs of northern California, not to serve as a guide to the whole kit and caboodle (whatever a "caboodle" might be). I hope you realize that to a hard-core bugster like me, every single one of those 20,000 species has the potential to be wonderfully interesting in its own right. In other words, this book is supposed to be more inspiring than scholastic.

Before launching into the bugs themselves, let's take a moment to orient ourselves to the northern portion of the state of California. California is longer than it is wide, and it runs along the West Coast of the United States from the Mexican border in the south to Oregon in the north. Anything north of the San Francisco Bay Area is generally considered to be northern California, and in most respects it is more like Oregon than the southern part of the state. Along the coast, the terrain is mostly mountainous, more so the farther north one goes. These mountains are collectively referred to as the Coast Ranges, and within them one finds the legendary redwood forests, one of the features that make northern California such a magical place. Inland from the coastal mountains, running roughly through the middle of the state, there lies the Central Valley, a relatively low and flat area used primarily for agriculture. To the east, more mountains run north and south through northern

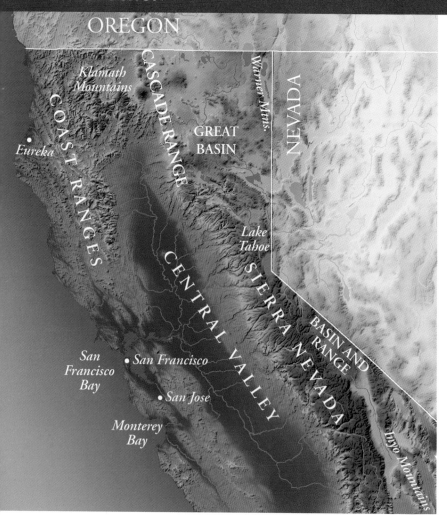

California. The Cascades in the north blend into the Sierra Nevada farther south, with the Klamath and Warner mountains up near the Oregon border, north of the Central Valley. This combination of topographic variety, the contrast between coastal and inland habitats, and the latitudinal span of the region give northern California a very diverse bug fauna, with plenty of exciting possibilities for the bugsters among us. And although the Bay Area is one of the most densely populated portions of North America, there are still many places in northern California where a bugster can feel almost alone, so long as you can shake the notion that Bigfoot might be watching both you and the bugs...

BASIC BUG BANTER

LIKE ANY science, the study of bugs has its own jargon. Some of its words have plain-language equivalents, but others do not. Unavoidably, then, it is important to get the gist of things before going on to read more about the bugs themselves. I suppose I could have presented this section as a glossary, but I think it will be more interesting as a sort of condensed textbook. I hope you agree.

Bug Structure

Let's start with the structure, or anatomy, of bugs, and let's also start at the front end of an average full-grown specimen. All bugs have a **head**, and on the head there are almost always **eyes** (with either one lens or many), a **mouth**, a set of appendages called **mouthparts** and a pair of feelers called **antennae** (one is an **antenna**). Eyes with multiple lenses are called **compound eyes**; eyes with one lens are called **ocelli** (one is an **ocellus**). Insect mouthparts that are elongated and modified for sucking are called a **proboscis** (the plural is **probosces**) or, in some cases, a "rostrum."

On many bugs, the head is joined to the rest of the body by an obvious line or groove, and it is somewhat moveable on a flexible but very short

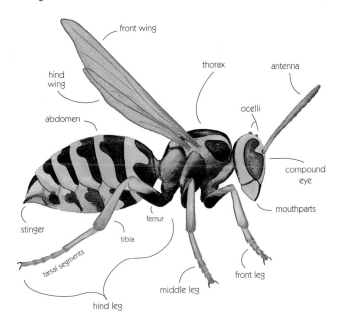

front wing

hind wing

thorax

antenna

ocelli

abdomen

compound eye

mouthparts

stinger

femur

tibia

tarsal segments

front leg

hind leg

middle leg

neck. On others (spiders and scorpions, for example), the head is part of a larger body part that also bears the legs—the **cephalothorax**. The head, thorax (or cephalothorax) and abdomen are often further divided into **segments** that may be easy to recognize on the surface.

Insects have a separate **thorax**; it is easy to recognize because each of its three segments—the **prothorax**, **mesothorax** and **metathorax**—bears a single pair of legs. If **wings** are present, they are borne by the middle and hind segments. Some insects, such as two-winged flies and some mayflies, have only one pair of flying wings, not two. In many groups, the thickened front wings serve as wing covers for the hind wings. The only part of a beetle's thorax that is visible from above is the prothorax, the top of which is called the **pronotum**.

Everything past the thorax is called the **abdomen**. At the tip of the abdomen, one finds the **anus**, the **reproductive structures** (**genitalia**) and, in many types of bugs, a rear-facing set of "feelers" called **cerci** (one is a **cercus**).

You might also notice **spiracles** on the sides of an insect's thorax and abdomen (openings for the multi-branched breathing tubes of the **tracheal system**) or **book lung openings** on the undersides of spiders, near the silk-producing **spinnerets**. Some **aquatic** insects (insects that live in the water) have **gills** as well, most of which are leafy or finely branched projections from the body. Scorpions have **pectines** (comb-like sensory appendages) on the underside of their cephalothorax.

LIFE HISTORY

Now let's discuss life history. Most bugs begin life as an **egg**. The egg then hatches into a baby bug, but not all baby bugs look like their parents.

Larva   *Pupa*   *Larva*

Pupa   *Larva (nymph)*   *Naiad (larva)*

Generally, if the newly hatched young look more or less like the adults (baby grasshoppers, for example), they are likely to be called **nymphs**. If the young are clearly different from the adults, the word **larvae** (singular is **larva**) is more widely used (although the larvae of butterflies and moths are called **caterpillars**). Some aquatic nymphs are called **naiads**, and spider babies are simply **spiderlings**. Entomologists have recently agreed to use the word "larvae" to refer to all sorts of immature insects, but they have to fight a long history of confusion to do so. If you think this is complicated, compare it to the situation with mammals, where you have to distinguish among pups, kids, calves, kits, foals, colts, lambs and so on.

As bugs grow, they have to shed their outer covering, which is called the **exoskeleton** (or more properly, the **exocuticle**), numerous times. Some bugs simply increase in size until they are large enough and mature enough to reproduce. Others show more obvious changes as they grow, the most common of which is the development of wings and **genitalia** (sexual parts). The genitalia of bugs are often complicated, involving hooks and claspers, as well as things that look like levers, pliers, syringes and the like. Sometimes the genitalia are visible from the outside and sometimes not. In spiders, one pair of mouthparts (the **pedipalps**) serves as the male sex organs, and in dragonflies and damselflies, the males have one set of genitalia at the tip of the abdomen and another at the base. The **base** of a structure, by the way, is always the place where it attaches to the rest of the body.

When a bug reaches the full-grown, ready-to-reproduce state, it is simply called an **adult**. However, for caterpillars and other grub-like larvae to become adults, they first have to enter into a resting stage, called the **pupa** (the plural is **pupae**), during which the amazing transformation takes place. Butterfly or moth pupae are sometimes called **chrysalides** (one is a **chrysalis**), and remember that the silk covering that some caterpillars make when they pupate, and not the pupa itself, is called a **cocoon**. Most cocoons are made by moth caterpillars, not butterfly caterpillars.

The change from young to adult is called **metamorphosis**, and there are three sorts. If the change is gradual, what we have is "**gradual metamorphosis**." If it involves the development of wings, or some other fairly major change in body form (but not a pupa stage), it is called "**incomplete metamorphosis**." If it involves a pupa stage, it is called "**complete metamorphosis**." These terms are old-fashioned, and, of course, there is nothing defective about an insect with "incomplete" metamorphosis.

Ecology

The **ecology** of bugs has to do with how they interact with other living things and with their non-living environment. The place where an insect lives is called its **habitat**, a word that means about the same as environment. Collectively, all of the plants and animals in a given habitat are called a **community**, and even larger such groupings are called **ecosystems**. An insect may recognize its habitat by soil type, by slope (or flatness), by altitude, by water characteristics (flow speed, dissolved oxygen, temperature and so on) or by the presence of specific types of prey or species of plants. When insects eat plants, the plants are called **host plants** or **food plants**, and the insects are called **herbivores**. If an insect drinks nectar, the plants are called **nectar plants**. Insects that eat other creatures are **predators**, and the creatures they eat are **prey**. If an insect lives on or inside a **host** animal, and either kills it very slowly or not at all, it is called a **parasite**. If it is a parasite only in the larval stage, it is called a **parasitoid**. If an insect eats things that are already dead, it is called a **scavenger**. If it eats poop, it is said to be **coprophagous**. Complex, isn't it? Also remember that a movement of bugs in many directions away from a given area is called **dispersal**, whereas movement in one shared direction is called **migration**.

There, that should do it for ecology. Now on to systematics.

Bug Systematics

Systematics is the study of how living things are related, in an **evolutionary** sense. In order to reconstruct the evolutionary tree of life, you really have to start with the basic unit of evolutionary change, the species. A **species** is group of living things that can interbreed among themselves in nature without **hybridizing** ("crossing") with other species—at least not *too* much. Species are grouped with other closely related species into **genera**, the singular of which is **genus**. Genera are grouped into **families**, families into **orders**, orders into **classes** and classes into **phyla**. This system is called the

Linnaean system of classification. The singular of phyla is **phylum**, and all of the critters in this book belong to one phylum, the **Arthropoda** or "joint-legged animals." These creatures are what I call "bugs."

Within the phylum Arthropoda, I have chosen examples from five classes: the crustaceans (Class **Crustacea**), the millipedes (Class **Diplopoda**), the centipedes (Class **Chilopoda**), the arachnids (Class **Arachnida**) and the insects (Class **Insecta**). The arachnids are further divided into four orders in this book: the spiders (Order **Araneae**), the harvestmen (Order **Opiliones**), the scorpions (Order **Scorpionida**) and the camel spiders (Order **Solifugae**).

Because of their great diversity, the situation with the insects is a bit more complex. We begin with insects with wings and incomplete metamorphosis, specifically the dragonflies and damselflies (Order **Odonata**), the mayflies (Order **Ephemeroptera**) and the stoneflies (Order **Plecoptera**). Next come the grasshoppers, crickets and such (Order **Orthoptera**, the **grigs**—the only English word for this group of insects—as more and more people are beginning to call them) and the cockroaches (Order **Dictyoptera**). Sucking bugs (the so-called "true" bugs) also experience incomplete metamorphosis, and they form the order **Hemiptera**.

The rest of the insects go through complete metamorphosis, which involves a pupa stage. They include the two-winged flies (the "true flies," Order **Diptera**), the wasps, bees and ants (Order **Hymenoptera**), the beetles (Order **Coleoptera**), the caddisflies (Order **Trichoptera**), the lacewings and ant lions (Order **Neuroptera**) and the butterflies and moths (Order **Lepidoptera**).

By the way, "**ptera**" means wing, "Hemiptera" means half-wing, "Diptera" means two-wing, "Lepidoptera" means scaly-wing and so on. If you look into the meanings of scientific names, it will help you remember them, but really, there is no substitute for simply memorizing the words and getting on with the more interesting aspects of entomology. Note as well that "species" is abbreviated as "**sp.**" (one) and "**spp.**" (more than one).

In most bug books, the various groups are presented in the order that I have just given. The closely related groups are thus

"Eyeball" Orb-weaver

19

placed together, beginning with those that are most **primitive** (in the sense of resembling the long-extinct common ancestor of the entire group) and ending with those that are most **derived** (a term that means they have undergone a great deal of evolutionary change). In this book, however, I have chosen to reverse the order. This arrangement still keeps related species together and gives you all the insight that the traditional order does, but it also allows you to start with butterflies and moths, rather than primitive wingless insects. My goal is to get you to like these animals, so I have chosen to begin with the niftiest ones. At the end of the insects, however, I have "artificially" grouped a number of unrelated aquatic insects together because that is the way many entomologists think of them—as a unit. The non-insect bugs follow the aquatic insects.

BEING A BUGSTER

This book is not about pests and how to kill them. Sure, some bugs are harmful, and I don't object to fighting back against them when the need arises, so long as no other species, such as people, are caught in the cross-fire. In fact, you'll find that some of my favorite bugs are pests.

Most bugs, however, are harmless, and all good bugsters know that they are the very backbone of the ecology of northern California, responsible for everything from pollination to decomposition, soil formation, regulation of other bugs and "weeds," food for birds and mammals and much more. Without apology, I think that all bugs are worthy of admiration and respect and at least a passing glance. If you don't understand bugs, you really don't understand the world in which you live.

Bugs are easy to find, at least on warm days during bug season, which means roughly March through October. This long season leaves us with only four months in which bugs are hard to find, which in my opinion is pretty darn good. Of course, May through September is the best time for bugs, during which time they are downright hard to miss. Bugs live in almost every conceivable habitat, from the alpine tundra on the tops of the highest mountains to the driest prairie sand dune, the insides of caves, the insides of our homes and every place in between.

Still, if you want to go out searching for bugs, I suggest looking for them in habitats such as these:

1) under rocks and boards (and remember to put the rocks and boards back once you look),

2) on plants and especially on flowers and the undersides of leaves,

The author and his son, bug-watching

3) at lights at night (but not the yellow bug-free lights),

4) in the water, especially where there are lots of water plants,

5) on bare sandy ground, even if it is far from water and

6) at various sorts of "bait."

My favorite bug baits include various mixtures of beer and sugar, painted on trees for moths and butterflies, as well as less appealing things, such as dung and carrion. Don't feel bad if you choose to ignore the bug-baiting option—after all, many sorts of bait are downright unhygienic. Remember not to touch the bait, and always wash your hands afterward— something my mother used to tell me often when I was a junior entomaniac.

In general, bugs like warm weather more than cool, and they are easier to find in sunny places than in the shade. They prefer humid days to dry, but they don't do much in the rain. Warm nights will bring out many flying insects, such as moths, but cool ones will not. During a full moon, bugs are less attracted to lights. Wind does not necessarily deter bug activity, but it certainly makes them harder to find and to follow. Daytime bugs get going well after we have breakfast, and they slow down appreciably by around dinner time.

The easiest way to get a close look at a bug is to catch it and examine it—then let it go. Nets are easy to make, and good ones are also inexpensive to buy through mail-order. Small bugs can be placed in clean jars for a brief

A Nikon 5T lens on a pair of binoculars

period, and large ones, such as butterflies and dragonflies, can be gently examined while still in the net. Many can be handled gently. In my opinion, this approach is the overall best way to study bugs, and it gives a great deal of satisfaction for very little effort. All of the suggestions that follow involve both more work and more of a commitment to mastering unusual techniques.

If you want to watch bugs without disturbing them, you can do it the old-fashioned way, on your elbows with a Sherlock Holmes magnifying glass, or you can try other sorts of optical tools. Close-focusing monoculars are very useful for bug-watching, and I recommend them very highly, although they are sometimes hard to find. You might also try a pair of compact binoculars, such as the Bushnell Natureview 8 × 30, with a Nikon 5T close-up lens held in front of them (total cost about $200–$250). This way, you get a clear view of the bug, at a distance of about $1^1/_2$ feet, with both eyes at once.

Depending on what sort of bug you choose to watch, you may need to modify your style. When I watch tiger beetles, for example, I find myself crawling around on the sand, continually moving to follow my subjects. On other occasions, I often place a small folding chair in front of a buggy-looking plant and then sit in one place while scanning the flowers, leaves and stems for interesting creatures on which to spy.

Bug-watching teaches us a lot. Because the behavior of many of our local bugs is poorly known, any of us has the ability to make useful observations once we have learned to identify the creatures we are encountering. On the other hand, simply immersing yourself in the lives of insects and other buggy critters is a wonderful way to make a deep and moving connection with the non-human world all around us. You can be as scientific or as recreational as you want.

If you make detailed observations of particular sorts of insect, it is probably a good idea to collect a few "voucher specimens," so other bugsters can confirm your identifications after the fact (for really easy identifications,

a close-up photograph will also suf-
fice). When I was young, the *only*
way to approach bug study was to
make a collection. Collecting is still
allowed almost anywhere except in
national and state parks, but it is less
popular now than it was a few
decades ago.

If you choose to make a collection for educational or scientific
reasons, remember to limit your
catch, treat every specimen with
respect, take the time to label,
arrange and store the specimens
correctly, and plan to donate them to
a university or museum once you are
done with them. Instructions for
insect collecting are easy to come by,
and, for the most part, you will
encounter ill-will only when you collect and kill butterflies and moths—
most people feel little sympathy for
other sorts of bugs.

Increasingly, however, bugsters are polarizing into collecting
and anti-collecting camps. I wish
they weren't, but because they are, I
want to briefly discuss the matter.
Collectors claim they do not harm
bug populations: bugs generally
have short generation times and
high reproduction rates, and they
recover from "harvest" much more
easily than vertebrates. Collectors
also point out that the identities of

pinned specimens can be confirmed, whereas sightings alone are always subject to doubt. Anti-collectors, on the other hand, are reluctant to admit that
collecting is always innocent, because they believe it *must* be possible for a
large enough group of collectors to cause local extinctions of small isolated
"colonies" of rare bugs. These types are exactly the sorts of bugs that many

An entomologist with a research collection

collectors seek, so this fear could be well-founded if collecting were ever to become truly popular (which in itself seems unlikely). Unfortunately, these isolated populations also become places where collectors and anti-collectors come into uncomfortable proximity with one another, at which point it is very difficult for the watchers to do their thing with collectors chasing the very bugs they want to observe, and vice versa.

When I try my hardest to be rational about this subject, it seems obvious to me that insect collectors are not a big threat to the insects of northern California. In fact, I believe they are inconsequential. Logging, pesticides and habitat destruction are all of much greater concern. It seems to me that the real core of the collector/anti-collector debate has to do with two rather unscientific human motives. First, no one likes having their freedom (or the freedom of their favorite bugs) restricted, especially when no laws exist to back the restrictions up. Second, collectors and anti-collectors seem to dislike the sorts of people that the opposing group represents. Looking at these motives, let's admit that it is difficult to sympathize with those who kill the very objects of their passion. At the same time, it is difficult to take a person's scientific motives seriously when they are willfully unsure of the identities of the creatures they are observing and could easily remedy the situation by catching a few. It also seems clear to me that peer pressure has a great deal to do with the attitudes of individual bugsters—in a group of watchers, no one dares bring out a net; among collectors, the binoculars stay in their cases.

As for my personal approach, I usually go out with nothing but binoculars and a camera, content to watch and admire. When I'm doing something scientific, I also take a net. I sometimes collect a specimen or two, but most of the time I use institutional collections for research. I still find many uses for pinned insects (for example, when writing this book), but I no longer feel a deep-seated need to possess them for myself. I try to act respectfully

Good insect photography equipment is now inexpensive and easy to use.

toward bugs whenever I can, but I'll admit that it is difficult to avoid inconsistency when swatting mosquitoes or splattering bugs on a windshield one moment, then treating certain bugs like endangered panda bears the next. The way I see it, this sort of "hypocrisy" is inescapable, and one can use it to either justify a callous attitude toward bugs, or accept it and atone by acting kindly toward them whenever possible.

Another fascinating bugster activity is insect rearing, which is much less controversial than collecting or watching—people who rear bugs are more or less forced to treat them with loving care, and they will inevitably acquire a specimen or two through accidental mortality. Most often, when people want to rear bugs, they start with some caterpillars and see what type of butterfly or moth they will turn into. To rear caterpillars, put them in a well-ventilated cage and provide them with plenty of leaves to eat. Place the cut stems in water with some means of preventing the caterpillars from drowning in the water supply (I place soft foam around the stems). When they are ready, some caterpillars pupate above ground, but for those that dig into the soil, make sure they have some potting soil or peat to dig in when the time comes. If the pupae don't hatch in a couple of weeks, place them in the refrigerator for the winter, and mist them with water every few days (refrigerators are terribly dry places). Take them out in the spring, and don't be surprised if sometimes you end up with parasitic flies or wasps rather than butterflies or moths. Rearing caterpillars is not easy—as they grow they require more and more fresh food, and their quarters need to be cleaned frequently. If you have a lot of them, they can be almost as much effort as a new puppy!

For other insects, you will have to be more creative with your rearing techniques, but more information on this subject is becoming available all the time. Temperature, humidity, food and light, as well as making things escape-proof, are all subjects you will have to consider carefully with each new species that you try. Another popular thing to do is to set up a pond aquarium, much the same way as setting up a tropical fish tank, but without a heater.

And remember, if your bugs don't look healthy, take them back to where you caught them and let them go.

Of course, you should not forget the potential of bug photography or even bug drawing. These activities require specialized equipment, and a certain amount of practice, but there are plenty of good books on the market that can help you. With more and more sophisticated photo equipment available all the time, professional quality bug photography is now possible with everyday equipment that you buy at an average camera store.

THE 125 COOLEST
BUGS
of
NORTHERN CALIFORNIA

WESTERN TIGER SWALLOWTAIL

Papilio rutulus

T he Western Tiger Swallowtail is a creature of late spring and early summer. This big, bright butterfly is impressive to watch, with its soaring wing-beats and graceful lines. Swallowtails are also among the few butterflies with attractive bodies—they are streamlined and luxuriantly furred in yellow and black—and even without their extravagant wings, they would be noteworthy bugs. The "tails" on a swallowtail's hind wings are there so that birds will grasp them and fly away with a beak full of membrane rather than the butterfly itself. Often, you will see a swallowtail with one or both tails missing.

There are five species of closely related North American "tiger" swallowtails, and the most famous is probably the Eastern Tiger Swallowtail (*P. glaucus*). In that species, some females are black, to mimic the distasteful Pipevine Swallowtail (*Battus philenor*). Here in California, however, all female Western Tiger Swallowtails are yellow like the males, despite good numbers of Pipevine Swallowtails in this area. The poplar-feeding caterpillars of the Western Tiger Swallowtail are amazing in their own right, with a fake snake head emblazoned on a smooth, green body. The fake head draws attention away from the real head, which is small and unimpressive to look at.

WINGSPAN: about 3.3 in.
HABITAT: along watercourses and in gardens.

PALE SWALLOWTAIL
Papilio eurymedon

Pale Swallowtails aren't really pale; they are white. Or, more accurately, they are creamy white and black. Because their close relatives in the tiger swallowtail group are all yellow and black, some people consider them "pale" by comparison, which really isn't fair. These big, bright butterflies are downright elegant, with a soaring flight style and graceful lines. While they sip at a flower, they tremble their wings nervously and dance on their slender, black legs. They can flutter as lazily as any butterfly, or they can "put it in gear" and fly amazingly fast, with powerful, athletic wingbeats.

The Pale Swallowtail is easy to distinguish from the Western Tiger Swallowtail (p. 28) and the Two-tailed Swallowtail (*P. multicaudatus*), not only by color but by its wide, dark wing borders as well. More than any other swallowtail, the Pale Swallowtail is characteristic of the western United States. This hilltop butterfly prefers the high ground, and it seems to like

WINGSPAN: about 3.3 in.
HABITAT: hilltops and clearings.

dry areas more than wet ones. The caterpillars, which feed mainly on ceanothus and cherry leaves, are typical for tiger-type swallowtails: greenish, with a false snake head pattern on the thorax.

CABBAGE WHITE
Pieris rapae

Our least-loved butterfly is a European immigrant, and its caterpillars love nothing better than to drill through defenseless greens in a suburban vegetable garden. When Europeans brought their vegetables here from the Old Country, they brought this butterfly, too. For many people the "cabbage moth" is the most familiar butterfly of all, and it is certainly common in the suburbs and in other places where native butterflies rarely venture. Up close, it is not a bad-looking creature, with subtle greens and yellows on a background of milky white.

The color of Cabbage Whites is a warning to birds that these butterflies taste bad, but because most of our Cabbage Whites grow up in gardens rather than among toxic wild weeds, they actually taste just fine. The similar Margined White (*P. marginalis*) lives throughout the region (except for the Central Valley), almost exclusively in natural areas and forests, where its caterpillars feed on wild members of the mustard family. Happily, it seems that the Cabbage White and its native cousin stay out of each other's way—the country white and the city white, so to speak.

WINGSPAN: about 2 in.
HABITAT: gardens and agricultural areas.

ORANGE AND CLOUDED SULPHURS
Colias eurytheme & C. philodice

Sulphurs are so named because most of them are yellow. For this reason, they may also be responsible for the name "butter-fly." The Orange Sulphur and the Clouded Sulphur are almost identical on the underwing. On the upper wing surfaces, however, the Orange is orange, and the Clouded (illustrated above) is yellow. Both are butterflies of open, sunny meadows and fields, as well as mountaintops and clearings. They have a direct, powerful style of flight that really doesn't fit into the category of "fluttering." Flowery fields, where they sometimes fly in the thousands, are great places to find sulphurs of all sorts. These two sulphurs go through at least two generations during a typical butterfly season. The first ones to emerge are not the earliest butterflies of spring, but the last survivors are often the last butterflies of fall.

WINGSPAN: about 2 in.
HABITAT: open areas.

Over most of our area, the Orange Sulphur is the most common species of sulphur, and where additional species occur, other than the Clouded, identifying them can be a tricky chore indeed. In fact, some of the sulphurs are probably the toughest butterflies of all to identify correctly.

31

CALIFORNIA DOGFACE

Colias eurydice

The California Dogface is the official state insect of California, and in my opinion it deserves a better name! It is a shame that butterfly experts didn't settle on "Flying Pansy," another common name for this spectacular insect. But why "dogface"? The name refers to the light areas on the inner surface of the front wings—they resemble the faces of two poodles, looking outward. (At least to some people they do.) On females, the "poodles" are yellow, but on males they are partly iridescent purple.

Among the sulphur butterflies, to which the California Dogface is related, iridescent purple is a very rare color, but it does make sense. Many male sulphurs have patches of wing scales that reflect ultraviolet light, which we cannot see. Ultraviolet means exactly what it says: "ultra-violet," or "beyond the wavelength of violet light." For the California Dogface, the patches have shifted ever so slightly in hue so that they are now visible to the human eye. Thus, in this species alone, we see the brilliant displays

WINGSPAN: about 2.4 in.
HABITAT: foothills of the Sierra Nevada and Coast Ranges.

that male sulphurs present to their prospective mates. Unfortunately, as you will soon notice if you go in search of them, California Dogfaces almost never open their wings when they are at rest, making the shining purple poodles a rare sight indeed.

SPRING AZURE
Celastrina ladon

Bluebirds are fine for some, but for those who love the smaller creatures, there is no more uplifting sight than the year's first Spring Azure. Flashing and dodging, close to the ground, this lovely little butterfly is as iridescent as a tropical parrot and as bright as the spring skies above. Later in the season, other species of "blues" will appear, with darker blue

WINGSPAN: about 1 in.
HABITAT: forest clearings and open areas.

colors and more crisply marked underwings, but the Spring Azure is the one that comes out first, making it the species we know and love the best.

In fact, the Spring Azure is usually the first butterfly of the year to emerge from its pupa. Most of the other spring butterflies, such as Mourning Cloaks (p. 39) and Tortoiseshells (p. 40), have spent the winter as adult butterflies, tucked away under bark or among deadfall. By the time late spring rolls around, the last of the azures are looking gray and weather-beaten. Most butterflies live only a week or two as adults, and their brief lives are usually squandered at the expense of their diminutive beauty. It is the male azures we see most often, because they fly whenever the sun is out, searching for females.

PURPLISH COPPER

Lycaena helloides

Anyone who takes an interest in butterflies will soon find that the subject is inexhaustible. Just when you think you have encountered all of the butterfly types in your area, you notice a small, inconspicuous one, low to the ground. Most of the time, this butterfly will be a copper, and it is a delight. Most of our coppers are at least partly orange, and a combination of orange and brown markings does, indeed, give them a semi-coppery look, but none of the coppers look as much like copper as a good copper-colored beetle.

The most common species of copper in our area is probably the Purplish Copper, and it is the males that have a purple iridescence. Other species of coppers generally share the same color pattern and can be more or less orange, though the Mariposa Copper (*L. mariposa*) is

WINGSPAN: about 1 in.
HABITAT: open areas and clearings, especially moist ones.

mottled brownish gray on the underwing, and the male Blue Copper (*L. heteronea*) is bright blue on the upper wing—not "copper" at all. The Purplish Copper first appears in April, and it can produce two or three generations in a season. Purplish Coppers are often seen in suburban neighborhoods.

HEDGEROW HAIRSTREAK
Satyrium saepium

Hairstreaks are related to coppers and blues, and like them they are small butterflies with deep black eyes surrounded by a white border. This distinctive look makes all members of the gossamer-winged butterfly family easy to recognize. The Hedgerow Hairstreak, like many coppers, is, well, coppery on the upper wing surface, but it is not common for this butterfly to spread its wings, so it is the underwings we see most often. Like other hairstreaks, the Hedgerow Hairstreak has a tiny tail on the margin of each hind wing. When the hind wings are slowly rubbed together, the little tails slide past one another and look like antennae. Apparently, birds are often fooled by this tactic, and so they bite at the wrong end of the butterfly. Many hairstreaks also have colorful spots at the bases of the tails—they serve as a false head in

WINGSPAN: about 1 in.
HABITAT: dry shrubs or forests in hilly country.

order to enhance the antenna effect—but the Hedgerow Hairstreak seems not to need this decoration. Perhaps its brownish color works as camouflage, which might be compromised by brighter markings.

Like other hairstreaks, this species overwinters in the egg stage. And, like many other butterflies and moths, its caterpillars feed mainly on ceanothus plants, which are also called "wild lilac." The flowers of the ceanothus also provide nectar for the adult hairstreaks, as do goldenrod and other wild blossoms.

HYDASPE FRITILLARY

Speyeria hydaspe

The Hydaspe Fritillary is a typical "greater fritillary," a group of medium-to-large, orange-and-black butterflies. On the underside of the hind wings, most greater fritillaries have a dazzling array of bright silver spots. Butterflies see things differently than people, and much of what they see lies in the ultraviolet range, so these spots are brilliant ultraviolet beacons to other fritillaries. At a distance, fritillaries attract one another with their appearance, but when they get close, they choose to communicate with perfumes instead. Sound familiar? Hydaspe Fritillaries, however, have underwing spots that are not silver, and they can even be a buffy brown. But still, they find their mates, thus proving that there are many successful strategies for courtship, even among bugs.

WINGSPAN: about 2.2 in.
HABITAT: open areas in the mountains.

Fritillary caterpillars, by the way, feed on the leaves of violets, and they come out only at night. In mid-summer, when the air is filled with fritillaries, but the violets have finished blooming, you wouldn't think there were enough violet leaves to go around. For bugsters who like identification challenges, the greater fritillaries fit the bill perfectly. There are many species in our area, and some of them are so similar to one another that even experts can't seem to agree on what names to use.

PACIFIC FRITILLARY
Boloria epithore

Fritillary is a confusing word. It refers to a large assortment of orange-and-black butterflies, and it can be pronounced either "FRIT-ill-erry," or "frit-TILL-err-ee." To make things more complicated, there are flowers called "fritillaries," and in Europe all sorts of semi-related butterflies are called "fritillaries" as well. The Pacific Fritillary is one of the so-called "lesser fritillaries." Lesser fritillaries are generally smaller than the greater fritillaries, and few of them have silver spots on their underwings as great fritillaries do (and the Pacific Fritillary has none).

A number of species of lesser fritillaries emerge throughout the butterfly season, and they are easy to find, because most of them have the enchanting habit of spreading their wings wide open to the sun while feeding. For this reason, they also make great subjects for nature photography. Some of these fritillaries live in meadows in forested areas, but others range far

WINGSPAN: about 1.4 in.
HABITAT: meadows and clearings; absent from the Central Valley.

into the alpine zone at the tops of mountains. To distinguish a Pacific Fritillary from the other lesser "frits," one has to memorize the exact pattern of splotches on the underside of the hind wing—a fairly standard thing to do once you become a hard-core "butterflier."

37

COMMON BUCKEYE

Junonia coenia

What a great name: "buckeye." Indeed, among the butterflies of northern California that have eye-spot patterns on their wings, this one is probably the most spectacular. The Common Buckeye is not particularly colorful—the wings are mostly brown, yellow and orange—but it still has an arresting effect on those who see it up close. The eye-spots themselves have more color than the rest of the wing, and they are shaded in blue. They are not particularly lifelike, but to us they are beautiful, and to bird predators they are startling. The eye-spots also gave the Common Buckeye the common name "Peacock" in some areas, but among butterfly enthusiasts the real Peacock is a European species of butterfly—not to mention an Asian bird. Fortunately, Common Buckeyes habitually perch right on the ground, with fully spread wings, showing off their eye-spots to the world.

The Common Buckeye seems to be especially fond of disturbed areas, such as vacant lots and weedy fields. Of course, these sorts of areas are more likely to contain patches of open ground, whereas natural landscapes are more fully vegetated. One common food plant for buckeye caterpillars is plantain, which also grows in such places. Various nectar-bearing flowers complete the scene, and in such places male buckeyes settle in and wait for passing females. In other parts of the U.S., there are additional species of buckeye, but here the Common Buckeye is our one and only representative of the group.

WINGSPAN: about 2.4 in.
HABITAT: weedy fields, usually with patches of open ground.

MOURNING CLOAK

Nymphalis antiopa

The Mourning Cloak is a big, heavy-bodied, spectacular butterfly. You can hope to see one almost any sunny day that the temperature rises above freezing, even in winter. The adults emerge in mid- to late summer, at which point they are at their most magnificent: maroon with yellow trim and blazing blue highlights, with a bark-colored pattern on the underside. After feeding for a week or so, they go into a temporary dormancy and then emerge to feed again in the fall. When the snow comes, they tuck in under a chunk of bark, a shutter or a fallen log, and they hibernate. Sometimes they die during hibernation, and you find their remains when you clean out the attic or the woodpile.

WINGSPAN: about 3.1 in.
HABITAT: openings in forested areas.

The first warm days of spring bring them back out of hiding, and that's when they mate and lay eggs. By the time early summer rolls around, a few are still on the wing—worn and tattered, with wing fringes white instead of yellow. A Mourning Cloak can live a full year, which is almost a year longer than most other butterflies.

CALIFORNIA TORTOISESHELL

Nymphalis californica

The name "tortoiseshell" refers to the resemblance of this species' wing color to the polished shells of hawksbill sea turtles. These shells were once used to make all sorts of decorative items in Europe (one often sees tortoiseshell toiletry items in museums) before people realized that the turtles were becoming endangered. The first butterfly to bear the tortoiseshell name was the Large Tortoiseshell (*N. polychloros*) of Europe, a species so similar to the California Tortoiseshell that the two were once considered one and the same thing.

California Tortoiseshells are best known for their fluctuating population numbers and for their migrations. In some years they are very common, but in other years they are rare. When they are common, their migrations can be spectacular. They generally fly to the higher mountains during the summer and to the lowlands in the fall. Adult butterflies spend the winter hiding under bark and in woodpiles. Some years, these migrations can take California Tortoiseshells all the way to the eastern states, and there small, localized breeding populations of them may persist for several years before dying off.

WINGSPAN: about 2.4 in.
HABITAT: wooded areas.

WEST COAST LADY

Vanessa annabella

This species inherited part of its name from a relative, the Painted Lady (*V. cardui*). There are three species of "ladies" in California, and with practice you can generally find all three in a good year's bugstering, although they are indeed all quite similar. The West Coast Lady is a butterfly of the lowlands, and it goes through a number of generations during the year. Along the coast, in warmer areas, it can be found all year. The caterpillars

WINGSPAN: about 2 in.
HABITAT: lowland gardens and vacant lots.

feed on mallows and nettles. Easy to rear, the West Coast Lady makes a good educational subject for the classroom. However, most teachers use the Painted Lady instead, because kits can be purchased for this species, complete with artificial diet and detailed rearing instructions.

Populations of the West Coast Lady fluctuate from year to year in a relatively dramatic way, like those of the other lady species. However, though the Painted Lady often stages massive migrations that blanket the continent in butterflies, the West Coast Lady mostly stays right where you would expect—on the West Coast. Some wander to the central states and southwestern Canada, but not in large numbers.

41

CALIFORNIA SISTER

Adelpha bredowii

California probably has more species of butterflies named after it than any other state, and they are all beauties, too. The California Sister is one of the best-looking butterflies in North America. However, it is also a widespread species, and the race that occurs to the east was once called the "Arizona Sister." Why "sister," I really don't know. In some books, the species is simply referred to as "The Sister," but butterfly people seem to have settled on using the name "California Sister," at least for the moment. In terms of its relationships, this species is closely related to the admirals, and at a distance it resembles the Lorquin's Admiral (*Liminitis lorquini*), which also has orange wing tips, but that are not as well delineated.

When a California Sister soars into view and then comes to rest on a tree leaf above your head, backlit by dappled sunlight, you can be sure that this is one of the finest butterfly sights to be had. I can still see my first California Sister in my mind's eye, resting on a bright green leaf with a massive redwood tree rising to the sky behind it. The caterpillar food plants are all trees (such as oaks), and the adults often sip aphid honeydew off tree leaves. They will also rest on the ground, with wings fully spread, and, like other admirals, they habitually sip at mud. Luckily, this species is at home in gardens and parks as well as in forests and canyons, so every observant Californian should have a good chance of seeing one.

WINGSPAN: about 3.3 in.
HABITAT: wooded areas.

COMMON RINGLET
Coenonympha tullia

Here we have yet another species of butterfly that was once named after California. The fact that it is no longer called the "California Ringlet" is not, however, an indication of any sort of anti-California bias among butterfly people. Rather, it is an indication of how difficult it has been to classify the ringlet butterflies (in the genus *Coenonympha*) of North America. What was once considered four species or more is now considered one, and although the California populations of the Common Ringlet are distinctive, they are considered a local race and not a full species, indicating that they can interbreed with their relatives elsewhere. The Californian Common Ringlet is much lighter in color than the other races of Common Ringlet, two of which also occur in northern California. To make things even more complicated, this "complex" of butterflies also extends to Europe, and thus the question of whether there is one widespread species— or two or more—is still being debated. The "ringlet" part of the name refers to the small, ring-shaped eye-spots on the wings, which are better developed in the other races of this species.

> **WINGSPAN:** about 1.8 in.
> **HABITAT:** grassy meadows and open, grassy woodlands.

Some people find this butterfly somewhat mothlike, but to me it is very "butterflyish," even if it is not very colorful. As it flits over the grasses where its caterpillars feed, it adds a great deal to a bright summer's day, or, for that matter, to any day from early spring to late fall.

MONARCH
Danaus plexippus

The Monarch is our most famous butterfly and one of our biggest as well. Most people know the story: the Monarch is a migrant, and our local population returns each winter to a few small areas in northern and central California, where they spend the winter alongside the rest of the Monarchs from the West Coast of North America. Not only that— the Monarchs we see here are descendants of the generation that overwintered the year before. No one quite knows how they find their traditional wintering grounds, having never been there, but they do. Sadly, many of their wintering areas are threatened by development. It is likely that the northern California populations of the Monarch all overwinter in their home state, but recently some entomologists have suggested that a portion of the West Coast Monarch populations may overwinter in northwestern Mexico, in areas that we have not yet discovered. Tagging Monarchs with identification numbers may help solve this riddle.

WINGSPAN: about 3.7 in.
HABITAT: open areas near milkweed.

Monarchs make this great migration against huge odds, but they are partly protected by their body chemistry. As a caterpillar, each Monarch feeds on the leaves of milkweed plants, and chemicals in the leaves make both the caterpillar and the butterfly distasteful to birds. The distinctive orange and black colors on the Monarch advertise this fact, and another butterfly copies them to help protect itself. It is, of course, the Viceroy (*Liminitis archippus*), but Viceroys are not found in northern California.

POLYPHEMUS MOTH
Antheraea polyphemus

When a Polyphemus Moth comes flapping in to the porch light, everyone takes notice. Many people assume this moth is a butterfly, because it is so amazingly beautiful. The antennae tell the real story—feathery or thin and pointy antennae all belong to moths, whereas butterflies have slender antennae with thickened tips. The antennae of male

WINGSPAN: about 4.3 in.
HABITAT: deciduous forests.

moths are not feelers but smellers, and they pick up the faint aroma of a female's perfume. Following the scent upwind, the male finds his mate in the dark.

When daylight comes, Polyphemus Moths generally roost with their wings above their backs. If a bird tries to peck at them, they suddenly spread the wings to expose the fake eyes on the wings. Most birds are startled by this display, but it doesn't fool every predator. Often, all you find of a Polyphemus Moth is a pile of wings on the ground in the morning. The name "Polyphemus" comes from a one-eyed giant in Greek mythology; too bad the moth has four fake eyes and two real ones, for a total of six. Polyphemus caterpillars, by the way, are bright green and shaped like an extended accordion, and they feed on such things as birch and dogwood leaves.

CALIFORNIA SILK MOTH
Hyalophora euryalus

About the same size as a Polyphemus Moth (p. 45), the California Silk Moth is much more common in California. Still, it is so spectacular that it is always a welcome surprise when one appears around people. Both moths are members of the family of giant silkworms (Saturniidae), a group that is related to but separate from the commercial silkworm of Asia. At one point, the possibility of using giant silkworms for making commercial silk was explored in North America. It turned out that they wrap too many leaves and messy knots into their cocoons, so the plan failed. Thus, the giant silkworms remain symbols of the wild.

WINGSPAN: about 3.9 in.
HABITAT: shrubby areas.

Adult giant silkworms are among the bugs that have no mouth and live off body reserves once they emerge from the pupae. If you find one of these moths, and it poops a light brown liquid, don't be alarmed. The liquid, "meconium," consists of the wastes left over from the transformation from caterpillar to moth. This moth is often misidentified as the similar Cecropia Moth (*H. cecropia*), which lives only in eastern North America.

HERA BUCK MOTH

Hemileuca hera

The buck moths are also members of the giant silkworm family, despite the fact that they are not particularly gigantic. They are, however, very boldly patterned in black and white, with furry bodies that usually have tufts of bright red and yellow hairs. Most often, people

WINGSPAN: about 2.4 in.
HABITAT: open, arid areas in the northeastern part of our area.

notice them as they rest on vegetation near ground level, frequently when they are in the act of mating. They are day-flying moths, and their flight is fast and frantic. The heat of the day is the time when they are most active. The caterpillars feed on various sorts of sagebrush leaves, and the hairs on their bodies can sting you if you touch them. The result is a temporary rash—a reminder that hairy caterpillars are not always safe to handle, no matter how cute they might appear. In other parts of the world, touching certain caterpillars can send you to the hospital.

The buck moths are the most diverse group within the North American branch of the giant silkworm moth family, and bugsters are still struggling to determine exactly how many species there are and how to classify them. With about 18 species, the American Southwest is the continent's buck moth hot spot.

SHEEP MOTH

Hemileuca eglanterina

The Sheep Moth is a type of buck moth (a member of the genus *Hemileuca*), and like others in this group, it flies by day. Older books place this species in a separate genus, *Pseudohazis*, because it isn't a typical-looking buck moth. It has broader wings and a slimmer body, and this combination makes the Sheep Moth look a lot like a butterfly at first glance. However, Sheep Moths have feathery antennae—a sure sign that they are moths and not butterflies—and although they are active during the day, they still rely heavily on chemical communication to find their mates (the antennae are used to smell for prospective partners).

Compared to the other three buck moth species in northern California, the Sheep Moth has a much more intricate wing pattern that has "sunburst" edges and thick, graceful, black lines through the wings. The Sheep Moth is highly variable in color: some individuals are almost pure black and white, but others are a deep orange overall. Color variation is common among moths and butterflies, and it can serve a number of different functions that are related mainly to courtship, camouflage or mimicry. In the case of the Sheep Moth, we still do not know which explanation is correct. Watch for the Sheep Moth in late summer on warm afternoons, flying high above the ground.

WINGSPAN: 2–2.6 in.
HABITAT: open areas.

WHITE-LINED SPHINX
Hyles lineata

Sphinx moths are named for the way their caterpillars adopt a pose something like the famous Sphinx of Egypt. Another name for this group is "hawk moths," based on their streamlined form and rapid flight. I prefer "sphinx," because moths, unlike hawks, are not predators. In fact, they feed on flower nectar. There are many sorts of flowers that open their petals and produce nectar at night in order to accommodate these nocturnal pollinators.

WINGSPAN: about 3.5 in.
HABITAT: widespread, from gardens to deserts.

The proboscis of a sphinx moth can be extraordinarily long—sometimes longer than the moth's body, sometimes twice as long or more! If you plant honeysuckle or similar flowers in your yard, you may find that the White-lined Sphinx moths will feed on their nectar alongside hummingbirds, even in broad daylight. Petunias are also a good nectar source for these moths.

The caterpillars of the White-lined Sphinx are huge, of course, and they never fail to attract attention as they march across roads and sidewalks on their way to a place to dig into the soil and form pupae. They usually have a characteristic black-and-green striped appearance, although they can be quite variable. They sometimes become so abundant that they make the highways slippery with their crushed bodies. At such times, once the surviving caterpillars have eaten all of their preferred food plants (which include many species of low herbs) they will devour all the vegetation they can find.

49

BIG POPLAR SPHINX
Pachysphinx modesta

A large female Big Poplar Sphinx probably has the heaviest body of any moth in northern California, and this species' caterpillar certainly qualifies as one of our biggest insects overall. The Big Poplar Sphinx is an uncommon find, and even experienced moth devotees are always thrilled when they see one. Most sphinx moths feed on flower nectar, but some, like the Big Poplar, are unable to feed as adults. These moths have no mouth, and in this way they resemble the giant silkworm moths (pp. 45–48).

The Big Poplar Sphinx's wings are fairly broad for a sphinx; they are patterned in subtle pastel hues, camouflaged on the front wings and smeared with blue and red on the hind wings. The outer border of the front wings is wavy, which undoubtedly helps camouflage this moth during the day. The eyes are difficult to see, hidden by the furry forehead and shoulders. Considered together, these features probably gave this bug its scientific name, which is often translated as "modest sphinx." This name brings up an important point: bugs do not seem to possess a self-image or anything we might recognize as an ego. At least, no one has ever produced any evidence to support the notion. Thus, without an ego, I doubt it is possible for any bug to be either modest, conceited or anything in between.

WINGSPAN: about 4.3 in.
HABITAT: forests with poplars.

TOMATO HORNWORM MOTH

Manduca sexta

The Tomato Hornworm Moth is another familiar large sphinx moth, and it often flies to lights at night. The adults feed at flowers. Although it is not a particularly colorful sort of sphinx, it does have six pairs of yellow spots along the sides of its abdomen. This is where the *sexta* in its scientific name comes from, referring to the number six (and not to sex, as one might perhaps think).

The big green caterpillar of this moth feeds on three familiar species of closely related plants: tobacco, tomato and potato. For this reason, it has also been called the "Tobacco Hornworm" (the "horn" is a brown or red structure on the top of the end of the abdomen). However, another species (*M. quinquemaculata*), which is closely related, also feeds on these plants, and the two have shared the names Tomato Hornworm and Tobacco Hornworm for so long that gardeners and entomologists can't seem to agree about which name applies to which species. If my colleagues weren't likely to criticize me for it, I'd call one the "Six-spotted Sphinx" and the other the "Five-spotted Sphinx." In cases like this, however, scientific names are superior to common names.

WINGSPAN: about 4 in.
HABITAT: widespread.

SNOWBERRY CLEARWING

Hemaris diffinis

Another name for this little creature is the "Hummingbird Moth," and a third is "Bumble Bee Moth." Sure enough, when the Snowberry Clearwing hovers in front of a flower, uncoils its long, beak-like proboscis and shows off its handsome colors, you can see why some people think they are looking at a bird. In bird field guides, this moth is usually the only insect that warrants a picture. More than one friend of mine has told me that the first time they saw one, they crept up for a better look and then felt a deep sense of dread, realizing they had no idea what sort of life-form they were looking at.

Of course, there is nothing to fear about these moths, and, in fact, they are quite delightful. These clearwings are members of the sphinx moth family, and they behave like most of their nocturnal cousins. Only their see-through wings and daytime habits set them apart from their relatives. Typical of sphinxes, the caterpillars feed on a variety of forest plants. The adults are on the wing mainly in May. There are two, possibly three species of very similar clear-winged sphinxes in our area, of which the Snowberry Clearwing is the most common.

WINGSPAN: about 1.6 in.
HABITAT: widespread.

52

EDWARDS' GLASSYWING

Pseudohemihylaea edwardsii

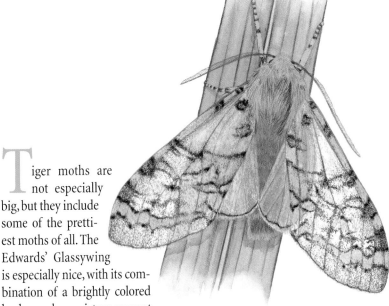

Tiger moths are not especially big, but they include some of the prettiest moths of all. The Edwards' Glassywing is especially nice, with its combination of a brightly colored body and semi-transparent wings. The wings are patterned with bands of dark scales when the moth first emerges from its pupa, but these bands wear off quickly, leaving the wings much more "glassy" in appearance. The Edwards' Glassywing is one of our largest tiger moths, and it is common in fall.

The bright colors of tiger moths warn predators not to eat them—they are filled with bad-tasting chemicals. Of course, their warning colors work only during the day. At night, when bats are their main enemies, they defend themselves in other ways. Some tiger moths can hear a bat's ultrasonic echolocation sounds, way above the range of human hearing, as it approaches. When a tiger moth feels threatened, it makes its own ultrasonic sounds to warn the bat that it is about to get a mouthful of bad-tasting tiger moth. Tiger moth caterpillars are generally fuzzy, and the fuzz can cause itchiness and rashes. They even weave these hairs into their cocoons, helping to ensure that they are protected at every stage of their life, both day and night.

> **WINGSPAN:** about 2.8 in.
> **HABITAT:** forested areas and gardens with oaks.

CARPENTERWORM MOTH

Prionoxystus robiniae

Two things set the Carpenterworm Moth apart from most of the other familiar moths of northern California. First, it shows "sexual dimorphism"; that is, the male looks different from the female. Second, its caterpillars eat wood, not leaves. The male Carpenterworm Moth is small and has streamlined, pointed wings, like a sphinx moth (pp. 49–52). As well, the male's wings are more darkly mottled than the female's, and his hind wings are yellow. The female (shown above) is larger, has broader wings and bears a translucent gray pattern. Most likely, the male is adapted to find the female from a distance, whereas the female is more of an egg-laying specialist. The caterpillars of this moth dig tunnels in the wood of deciduous trees, and, as you can imagine, they are large creatures. People often discover them when splitting firewood.

WINGSPAN: females about 2.8 in or more; males smaller.
HABITAT: coastal valleys and the Central Valley.

Moth specialists often divide the moths into the "macro-moths" and the "micro-moths," and, for the most part, the micros are indeed smaller than the macros. The Carpenterworm, however, is the biggest of our micros, and a big adult female can have a wingspan of 3.3 inches, dwarfing the vast majority of macro-moths. Such is the power of tradition, where unsuitable names persist despite their obvious flaws.

CALIFORNIA TENT CATERPILLAR MOTH

Malacosoma californicum

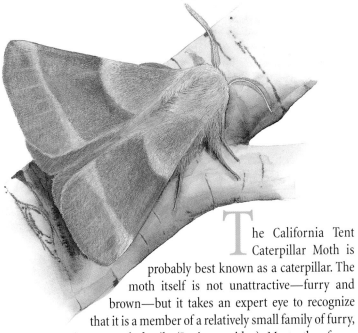

The California Tent Caterpillar Moth is probably best known as a caterpillar. The moth itself is not unattractive—furry and brown—but it takes an expert eye to recognize that it is a member of a relatively small family of furry, brown moths, the lappet moth family (Lasiocampidae). Most other furry, brown moths are members of either the owlet family (Noctuidae, p. 58) or the prominent family (Notodontidae, p. 57).

The California Tent Caterpillar Moth takes its name from the habits of its caterpillars. The mother moth lays her eggs all together in an egg mass, and when the caterpillars hatch, they stay together as a furry little family. They spin a silk shelter for themselves in which they spend the daylight hours safe from birds and parasites. At night they venture out to feed on leaves, usually of oak and fruit trees. When they are ready to pupate, they wander away from the tent and spin a cocoon about the size and shape of a perogy or a gyoza (Japanese dumpling). Some years there are huge numbers of tent caterpillars, and they can be important pests, but in other years they are rare. Parasitic flies and wasps, as well as diseases, cause these tremendous fluctuations in numbers.

WINGSPAN: about 1.4 in.
HABITAT: widespread in deciduous forests.

YARN MOTHS

Tolype spp.

T he Yarn Moths belong to the same family as the tent caterpillar moths (p. 55), but it is likely that most people would consider the Yarn Moths by far the more elegant of the two. A fresh specimen does indeed look a bit "yarnish," with long, bright white and brown hairs on its thorax and abdomen. This moth impresses people easily, because it looks so terribly warm and fuzzy. The hairs on the body seem to form a sort of mane, and the very hairy legs make this moth look like either a white tarantula or a Persian cat, depending on your sense of moth aesthetics. Almost all the Yarn Moths we see are males that have been attracted to lights.

WINGSPAN: about 1 in.
HABITAT: forested areas.

Yarn Moths are found in forested areas, because their caterpillars feed on tree leaves of various sorts. Oddly enough, some species feed on conifer needles, whereas others feed on deciduous tree leaves. In most groups of moths, closely related caterpillars feed on closely related plants, but this is not always the case, nor is it a tremendously mysterious phenomenon. The caterpillars of Yarn Moths are not economic pests.

ROUGH PROMINENT
Nadata gibbosa

The first thing most people notice about the Rough Prominent is its hairdo. On the top of its thorax, the hair-like scales come to a bit of a point, making the moth look a bit like a fuzzy, orange rockabilly player (use your imagination here). This species has also been called the "Tawny Prominent," because of its color, and the "White-dotted Prominent," because of the two white dots on the front wings. If you can remember all three names, you can probably recognize this moth without too much trouble. The scientific name of this species is also interesting, because *Nadata* has no meaning. The scientist who

WINGSPAN: about 2 in.
HABITAT: wooded areas in the Coast Ranges and the Sierra Nevada.

named it also named a related genus of prominent moths *Datana* simply by rearranging the letters in *Nadata*. For anyone who think all scientific names should be descriptive and meaningful, these moths provide a good counter-example, one that is fully allowed by the rules of zoological naming. After all, a name is just a label, and any other uses it may have are optional, not mandatory, or datmantory or nadattmory...

The caterpillars of the Rough Prominent are greenish, with a light stripe along their sides, and they feed on the leaves of oaks and other deciduous trees. Although some prominent moth caterpillars are quite unusual, with long filaments off the tail or spiked humps on the thorax, the Rough Prominent's caterpillars look quite "normal."

AHOLIBAH UNDERWING
Catocala aholibah

The underwings are moths of late summer. On occasion you see them by day, but for the most part they are creatures of the early evening, when they search for the sap-flows and over-ripe fruit on which they feed. Their coloration is remarkable, with camouflaged front wings and boldly colored hind wings. At rest, the Aholibah Underwing blends in perfectly with tree bark, closing its front wings over the hind ones. If a bird discovers it, the moth spreads its wings and takes advantage of the brief startle effect to allow it a moment in which to escape.

If you want to see one of these moths, here's what to do. Mix up a pot of beer, molasses, rum and lots of brown sugar. Warm it up to melt the sugar, then let it cool. Go outside and paint the mixture on the rough bark of poplar trees, then wait until after dark. Sneak up carefully with a flashlight, and try not to snap any twigs. These moths have good hearing, and they will sometimes flee at the slightest sound. Of course, after an hour or so of sipping the alcoholic bait, they seem less concerned about people and more absorbed in their own inebriated thoughts. This technique, by the way, seems to work much better in the eastern states than here in the West, much to the chagrin of local bugsters.

WINGSPAN: about 2.6 in.
HABITAT: deciduous forests.

DARWIN'S GREEN

Nemoria darwiniata

The relatively light body of the Darwin's Green struggles to flap its wings, and thus it doesn't whir in flight like most moths—it flutters. In fact, there are only three sure signs that this moth is not a butterfly. First, it has thin antennae with no clubs at the tips. Second, it flies by night. Third, it has a habit of crashing into leaves and branches when it flies, rather than deftly avoiding them.

Darwin's Green is called an "inchworm moth," because its caterpillars perform the familiar inching-along motion when they travel. Their method of locomotion is also responsible for the names "looper" and "spanworm." Many of this family, the geometers (Geometridae) are colorful, and

WINGSPAN: about 1.4 in.
HABITAT: forested areas.

some, like the Spear-marked Black (*Rheumaptera hastata*), fly by day. Almost always, when someone comes to me with a "butterfly that isn't in the field guides," it turns out to be a geometer. There are a number of similar species with green wings, but the Darwin's Green is one of the most common ones in our area.

PACIFIC TIGER BEETLE

Cicindela oregona

Tiger beetles are exciting: they have long legs, they run fast, they have powerful jaws for killing other bugs, and they also have large eyes. Some of them, as an added bonus, are brightly colored. The Pacific Tiger Beetle is widespread and common, but it is really one of the least colorful members of the group (see also p. 61). This beetle lives on moist sand and gravel, alongside both lakes and rivers. It generally likes open ground with few plants; in such places it finds it easy to spot prey and run it down.

It's a shame more people don't get a chance to see tiger beetles, but the reason is simple—the beetles always see us first. They are quick to take wing, but they usually don't fly far. It's easy to watch where they land and sneak up for a good look. If you watch a tiger beetle, you'll see it chase down food, zip out after potential mates and attack any small piece of debris that might be mistaken for an edible bug. These beetles come out only on sunny days, mind you, so don't go looking for them in the rain—that's the time to stick to water beetles.

LENGTH: 0.5 in.
HABITAT: widespread on river-banks and beaches.

CALIFORNIA TIGER BEETLE

Omus californicus

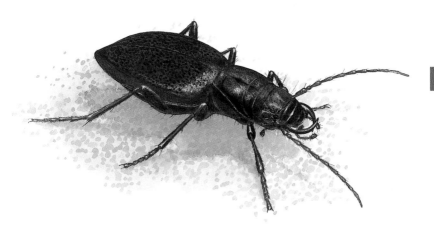

The tiger beetles are a worldwide group, ranging in size and shape from tiny, big-eyed, tree-dwelling species to huge, long-jawed, nocturnal tigers in South Africa. The California Tiger Beetle is a sort of missing link. Acting more like a ground beetle than a tiger beetle, with its nocturnal habits and a much slower running speed, it lives in vertical burrows in the ground and ambushes small bugs that walk by, rather than running them down. It is also colored like a ground beetle, being all black, with no white markings or iridescence, and it has small eyes and no wings.

LENGTH: about 0.6 in.
HABITAT: forest clearings.

These similarities, plus others, have led many specialists to declare that the tiger beetles form a subgroup within the ground beetle family. However, the California Tiger Beetle also possesses a type of jaws that is unique to tiger beetles, and its larvae are very typically "tiger-beetlish" as well. No intermediate jaws or larvae are known, either living or fossil, to connect the tiger beetles and the ground beetles. Thus, it is also possible that the tiger beetles form an ancient lineage separate from the ground beetles. And the solution to the problem of classifying them may live right here, with the California Tiger Beetle and its kin.

LONG-FACED CARABIDS

Scaphinotus spp.

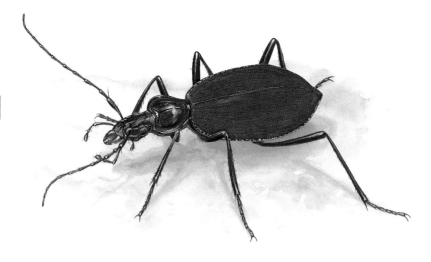

N ext time you are out camping in the moist coastal forests, spend a few extra minutes looking around with your flashlight when you make that inevitable trip to the outhouse after dark. Over much of the summer you can expect to find these large, brownish-black ground beetles prowling the forest floor. They are Long-faced Carabids, and they are elegant beetles indeed. With an elongated head, a remarkably slender prothorax and a body shaped like a cartoon rowboat, these are not your average ground beetles. Of course, there is no such thing as an average ground beetle, because in most places there are about as many species of ground beetles as there are kinds of birds. You wouldn't talk about an average bird, would you, halfway between a hummingbird and a pelican?

LENGTH: 0.8 in.
HABITAT: moist coastal forests.

Long-faced Carabids are thought to be adapted for eating snails and slugs—their long heads help them get into those hard-to-reach places inside snail shells and massive banana slug carcasses. However, the observations of local naturalists show that they will also feed on a variety of other small bugs, as well as on fallen fruit.

CATERPILLAR HUNTER

Calosoma scrutator

H ere is another sort of ground beetle, with its own fascinating story. Like the Long-faced Carabids (p. 62), this is one of the larger members of the family, but it differs from them in both its looks and its habits. Whereas the Long-faced Carabids like to rummage around just on the forest floor, the Caterpillar Hunter is both a ground forager and a fearless

> **LENGTH:** about 1.2 in.
> **HABITAT:** fields and relatively open, wooded areas.

climber of trees. Day and night, it explores the woods for its favorite food—caterpillars. Even fuzzy tent caterpillars are to its liking. With mighty jaws and a head as hard as a pebble, the Caterpillar Hunter can chew through a caterpillar's hairy defenses and gobble up the soft insides. These beetles can be found on the ground, in trees and bushes and at lights at night.

Another name for this species is "Fiery Searcher," which I prefer not to use, because it causes confusion with the Fiery Hunter (*C. calidum*). Other people call this caterpillar eater the "Green Hunter." Whatever the name, this is one of the most colorful of all ground beetles, but the colors are not really "fiery," unless you are thinking of those chemically treated pine cones that give off green and blue flames when you burn them.

63

BIG DINGY GROUND BEETLE

Harpalus pensylvanicus

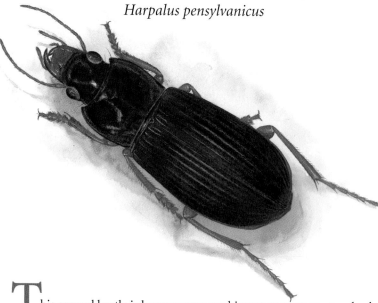

This ground beetle is by no means our biggest or most spectacular, but it is one that everyone should know. When you think that the average size of a beetle is about a tenth of an inch, the Big Dingy takes its rightful place as one of the whoppers.

In its appearance, the Big Dingy Ground Beetle is what biologists call "generalized." In other words, it doesn't possess any obvious body features that constitute adaptations for a specialized lifestyle (for example, the elongate head of a Long-faced Carabid, p. 62). This apparent lack of specialization does not mean that the Big Dingy is a primitive ground beetle—it is more likely that the Caterpillar Hunter (p. 63) resembles the long-extinct ancestor of the group. Because there are so many ground beetles, there have also been many people who made it their ento-mological mission to study them. Luckily, I have been able to meet many of the living "carabidologists" myself. There is a rumor among these people that the so-called "dingy" ground beetles (technically the "harpalines") were given their common name by specialists in other sorts of ground beetles, as a playful dig at those who study the "dingy" ones.

> **LENGTH:** 0.5 in.
> **HABITAT:** open, drier areas.

BURYING BEETLES
Nicrophorus spp.

Somebody has to deal with them, and you know exactly what I am talking about. Yes, I'm referring to dead mice. Without nature's help, the world would be knee deep in them. That is where the beautiful Burying Beetles (most are orange and black, though others are all black) fit into the grand scheme of things. Flying low over the ground, just before sun-

LENGTH: 0.6 in.
HABITAT: a variety of habitats; mostly open areas.

down, they spread their many-leaved antennae to the wind and sniff. They seek the unmistakable aroma of today's death. If they find a big carcass, such as a deer or a coyote, they join their buddies for a quick snack. On the other hand, if they find a dead mouse or some other tiny corpse, they rejoice.

A Burying Beetle's dream is to find a dead mouse and a mate all in the same evening. Then, the couple can bury their treasure, kill the maggots that might steal some of the meal and push the cadaver into a ball. They then lay their own eggs to start a family. The beetle grubs raise their little heads to beg for food, and in response Mom and Dad give them bits of putrescence to eat. Now isn't that nice? Who said that beetles don't possess the ability to show complex behavior and tender parental care?

DEVIL'S COACH HORSE

Staphylinus olens

The Devil's Coach Horse belongs to the large rove beetle family. Rove beetles typically have very short wing covers and elongated bodies, and they range from tiny scavengers to large predators. The Devil's Coach Horse is our largest rove beetle, and it is a predator par excellence.

Unfortunately, this is one of those bugs with a highly prejudicial English name, which it acquired in England before it was introduced to North America. "Devil's Coach Horse" is an interesting name, but a weird one. After all, this beetle doesn't look anything like a horse, and it doesn't make a habit of pulling things either, the way real coach horses do. Still, the thought of a pair of these beetles pulling a devil and his coach does bring to mind a spooky image. Of course, the devil in question would have to be very, very tiny. A rove beetle the size of a real horse would immediately fall to the ground, unable to get oxygen to its tissues because of its tracheal breathing system—a system that works only if the animal has a bug-sized body.

LENGTH: up to 1.2 in.
HABITAT: open areas.

MAY BEETLES

Phyllophaga spp.

The first thing to know about May Beetles is that you don't always see them in May. In fact, the various species in this group emerge throughout the warmer months. These beetles are the big, fat, clumsy, stupid ones that fly around at night and are strongly attracted to lights. So, when you are sitting outside after sundown, you often hear something like: "bzzzzh... bzzzahsssszzzzzzzzzzzzzzss... PFUT! bzt. bzt! Bzzzzzt!... bzzhsssss... bzt." That's the sound of a May Beetle on a collision course with the porch light, after which it falls on its back and can't find its feet. Kids like them, because they can find them in the morning (if hungry birds don't find them first), and they are fun to play with. They don't bite, because they don't eat once they become beetles. The grubs grow up underground, where they feed on roots for up to three whole years. On occasion, they are common enough here to be real pests.

LENGTH: 0.6–0.9 in.
HABITAT: forested areas.

May Beetles are members of the grand and glorious scarab beetle family, and they share with other scarabs such features as spiny legs, a sturdy body and many-leaved antennae.

TEN-LINED JUNE BEETLE
Polyphylla decemlineata

One of our largest scarab beetles, the Ten-lined June Beetle is related to the famous Sacred Scarab (*Scarabaeus sacer*) of Egypt that rolls balls of dung along the ground. The Ten-lined June Beetle, however, has no taste for dung. It belongs to a separate subfamily within the scarab group.

This June beetle quite naturally comes out mainly in July and August. The larvae live underground and, like other root feeders, are not a favorite of gardeners. The adults do not live long once they emerge, and they spend all of their time searching for mates and laying eggs. The antennae of the male in particular are awesome. They look a bit like moose antlers, but, being many-leaved, they give the impression of a bull moose with seven sets of antlers all stacked up on one another. When a male spreads this magnificent fan to the wind, the scent he seeks is that of the female. The color pattern of this beetle is also fascinating. If you look closely, with a magnifying glass, you'll see that the stripes on the wing covers are made up of tiny, overlapping scales. The scales are pointed at one end and rounded at the other; some are white, and the others are tan. They are set in a background of amber-colored cuticle, and each scale is as polished as a piece of hard wax.

LENGTH: 1 in.
HABITAT: widespread.

RAIN BEETLES

Pleocoma spp.

T he Rain Beetles are another sort of scarab, as you can tell from their antennae. With the first heavy rains of fall, male Rain Beetles emerge from the ground and fly around noisily in search of females. This pattern is common for many insects—hot, dry conditions are dangerous, because insects dehydrate easily. A bit of rain brings up the humidity and reduces the threat. Then, the male Rain Beetles pop out of their pupae and

LENGTH: about 1 in.
HABITAT: forested areas.

take to the skies. They prefer to fly at dusk and in the early morning, when conditions are especially cool and moist. Lacking wings, female Rain Beetles live in burrows in the ground, where they patiently wait for the males to find them by smell. The larvae also live underground, where they feed on the roots of deciduous trees, as well as on Douglas-fir.

Amazingly, a Rain Beetle larva can take up to 13 years to complete its development before pupating. There are many species of Rain Beetles, and biologists have been amazed at how their geographic ranges appear to be both localized and non-overlapping—no one area has more than a single species of Rain Beetle.

GOLDEN JEWEL BEETLE
Buprestis aurulenta

Among people who love beetles, another famous family is the metallic wood-borers. Scientists call them "buprestids," and they are also known as "jewel beetles." Many of these insects are large and iridescent, and they are almost robotic in their movements. They thrive in the heat of summer, and the best place to find them is on the sunlit sides of trees, where they meet their mates and lay the eggs that will become their "flathead-borer" larvae.

The Golden Jewel Beetle is one of the finest metallic wood-borers in northern California. It is widespread, because its larvae live inside dead or dying conifers. The adult beetle is a lovely iridescent green, with shining orange trim all around the wing covers. Once you learn where to look for them, you'll find jewel beetles in most places that have trees (and even some that don't). The colors of the Golden Jewel Beetle are unmatched by any other buprestid species in our area, but the buprestids are a worldwide family. In the tropics there are big, beautiful species that make ours look puny by comparison. In Southeast Asia, many of the most colorful buprestids are often made into real jewelry, set in gold with their legs removed, and sold for a high price.

LENGTH: 0.7 in.
HABITAT: forests with coniferous trees.

SCULPTURED PINE BORER
Chalcophora angulicollis

The Sculptured Pine Borer is another species of buprestid, our largest, and what it lacks in color in comparison to the Golden Jewel Beetle (p. 70), it makes up for in texture: it looks like it has been hammered out of bronze. The texture of the wing covers of this species makes this beetle difficult to see as it sits exposed on the bark of a pine tree, but when this insect flies, it is very noisy. Sometimes, listening for these bugs along a forest edge can be the best way to find one. They will also come to recently felled trees, because their larvae develop under the bark and in the heartwood of freshly dead conifers. They take a number of years to complete their development before pupating and emerging as adults.

LENGTH: 1–1.2 in.
HABITAT: forests with coniferous trees.

There are six species in the genus *Chalcophora* in the United States and Canada, and they are all big, spectacular beetles. If you find a buprestid that looks a lot like a *Chalcophora* but is about half the size, it is probably a member of the related genus *Chrysobothris*, with more than 130 species in North America north of Mexico. Like almost all other insect groups, the buprestids can provide an endless amount of fascination, and getting to know them all can easily fill a lifetime with interesting adventures. The fact that so few people choose to pursue such an interest has nothing whatever to do with how rewarding it can be.

WESTERN EYED CLICK BEETLE

Alaus melanops

The Western Eyed Click Beetle is the largest member of the click beetle family on the West Coast. It is instantly recognizable not only by its size but also by the two eye-spots on its pronotum. Because this beetle lives mostly in rotten wood and under bark, the eye-spots probably serve to startle predators that discover it while searching in these places. Many people call this species the "Eyed Elater."

The click beetles are a diverse family, and most of them are confusingly similar in a generally brown and featureless way. Still, they all share the amazing characteristic that gives the family its name—the "click." Turn one over on its back, and it flails with its legs for a moment or two. Then, it arches its body, and suddenly—PUNG!... it flips end over end into the air, and, like a tossed coin, it lands back on its feet roughly half the time. The truth is, however, that these beetles probably do not click as a result of this action. In nature, it is doubtful that they fall on their backs on a perfectly flat surface very often. Instead, the click probably functions to startle predators, and some types of click beetles can use the click to launch themselves into the air even if they are not upside-down.

LENGTH: about 1.2 in.
HABITAT: dry forests.

STINK BEETLE

Eleodes hispilabris

During mid-summer in the drier parts of northern California, things can get a mite hot. So what in tarnation is a big black beetle doing, running around on the sun-baked ground during the heat of the day? The Stink Beetle seems to thrive in deserts, and its black color somehow doesn't make it heat up as much as we might think it would. In other parts of the world, some stink bugs can "drink" from moist air, early in the morning, simply by opening their anus to the breeze, before the sun comes up.

The Stink Beetle gets its name by doing head stands and puffing smelly gas out its back end if you disturb it. (Some beetles cheat, mind you, and do the head stand without the puff.) Because of this ability, Stink Beetles don't have much to fear from most predators, or they wouldn't be walk-

LENGTH: 0.5–1.5 in or more.
HABITAT: open, arid areas.

ing around in the open all day. These beetles are members of the darkling beetle family, a group that includes the familiar Meal Worm Beetle (*Tenebrio molitor*) that is often sold for pet food and fish bait.

73

ASH GRAY LADYBUG
Olla v-nigrum

When most people think of lady-bugs, they think of cute little beetles that are red and black. In fact, the "lady" part of their name (as in "ladybug," "ladybird" and "ladybeetle" and, in Europe, "ladycow," "ladyclock" and so on) is a reference to the Virgin Mary and a red cloak that she commonly wore, at least according to some schools of painters.

The Ash Gray Ladybug, of course, is not red at all; it is usually gray and black instead of red and black. It is still a ladybug, however, and, like its relatives in the ladybug family, it feeds mainly on aphids. It is commonly seen on the leaves of deciduous plants. Some Ash Gray Ladybugs are not ash gray at all, but instead they are mostly black, with a large pale patch on each

LENGTH: about 0.2 in.
HABITAT: plants with aphids on them.

wing cover. Many ladybugs show this sort of color variation, and it is the subject of a great deal of genetic and ecological study. There are some European ladybug species that begin life quite gray in color so that they can blend in with the dead leaves of winter while hibernating. When spring comes, these same beetles darken and become reddish, warning predators that they taste bad. Ash Gray Ladybugs, on the other hand, remain ash gray (or black) throughout their adult lives, showing that there are many successful ways in which a ladybug can be a ladybug!

CONVERGENT LADYBUG

Hippodamia convergens

The Convergent Ladybug is common in grassy fields, lawns and gardens. When identifying ladybugs, look at the color, the arrangement and number of spots, the pattern on the pronotum and the overall shape of the beetle. The thing that confuses some people is that a Convergent Ladybug is not just an older, bigger Two-spot Ladybug (*Adalia bipunctata*), but that it is a separate sort of critter altogether—a separate species.

Once ladybugs emerge from their pupae, they don't change their spots, nor do they grow in size. They also don't change their spots to predict weather, as some people once believed. What a strange view of nature! As if one creature exists only to help another one survive—the ultimate in self-lessness. Sorry, it just isn't true.

Another myth associated with these ladybugs is that if you buy them for your garden, they will control all your aphids. The ladybugs are collected in their mountaintop hibernation sites, and when you transport them and release them, most of them simply fly away or go back to sleep. They con-

LENGTH: 0.2 in.
HABITAT: open areas; hilltops in spring and fall.

gregate while they are hibernating (by the thousands, which makes them easy to harvest), but when they go looking for food, they don't like much company or competition.

75

CALIFORNIA PRIONUS

Prionus californicus

Who could blame an enthusiastic bugster for imagining that the California Prionus is our own version of the greatest longhorn beetle of all, *Titanus giganteus*. *Titanus* can be 6 inches long (older books often said it is the size of "a man's hand"), lives in South America and once merited its own article in *National Geographic*. I see nothing wrong with appreciating bugs for their resemblance to tropical relatives. After all, the only thing *Titanus* has that the California Prionus lacks is size, and the Prionus is not a small bug! Both the California Prionus and the tropical *Titanus* are leathery-brown, with big eyes, powerful jaws and a spiked pronotum—all features of their subfamily, the "prionines."

I first encountered this insect on my birthday, somewhere back in my teens. I was on a family vacation at Parksville, on Vancouver Island in British Columbia, lying sick in bed feeling sorry for myself. Then, the biggest beetle I had ever seen flew up and landed on the window screen. I couldn't catch it, but the intensity of that encounter made me forget completely about the flu and my assumption that it would be a lousy day, with no party and no cake. The appearance of that beetle made sure it was a birthday I would never forget.

LENGTH: up to 2 in.
HABITAT: western forests.

PONDEROUS BORER

Ergates spiculatus

The English name for this species, "Ponderous Borer," is a reference to the fact that it sometimes lives in ponderosa pine trees, not that it is "ponderous" in its own right. The Ponderous Borer is in most ways very similar to the California Prionus (p. 76), but notice that the Ponderous Borer has smaller spines on its pronotum and less comb-like antennae. Although these two insects are so similar, I couldn't resist including them both in this book, because they are the two largest beetles in our area.

As their name suggests, Ponderous Borer larvae most often do grow up in pine trees, but in truth any conifer will do. They do not feed in living trees, only in dead logs and standing snags. Thus, they are part of the fauna that contributes to the formation of forest soil and the turnover of plant matter in the ecosystem. You'd think that would make them economically neutral, along with the rest of the insect decomposers. However, foresters resent the "damage" they do to standing dead trees after a fire, making salvage logging less profitable for them. Bugs just can't seem to win sometimes. According to some sources, this beetle was actually the source of a very valuable gift to the logging industry: its chewing mandibles are said to have been the inspiration for the first chainsaw.

LENGTH: up to 2.4 in.
HABITAT: coniferous forests.

BANDED ALDER BORER
Rosalia funebris

The Banded Alder Borer is another longhorn beetle, but it has a very different look from the California Prionus (p. 76) and the Ponderous Borer (p. 77). The longhorn beetles are a very diverse family, and thus systematists have divided it into subfamilies, in which the genera are arranged. Hard-core bugsters learn to recognize the subfamilies of longhorns, along with the subfamilies of scarab beetles and ground beetles. So, the California Prionus is a prionine ("PRY-oh-nine"), and the Banded Alder Borer is a cerambycine ("serr-am-BISS-ine"). Many cerambycines have colorful wing covers, and the Alder Borer is one of the nicest. Bugsters sometimes call the whole family "bissids," an abbreviation of the technical term cerambycid ("serr-am-BISS-id").

The larvae of the Banded Alder Borer are wood-borers in deciduous trees, and the adults are often found on or near the trees themselves. They are also attracted to recently painted buildings, and sometimes they arrive by the hundreds. The antennae of the male Banded Alder Borer are longer than its body, and those of the female are shorter. As is usual among beetles, however, the female has a heavier body, because she is the one who carries the eggs.

LENGTH: about 1 in.
HABITAT: coastal forests.

BLUE MILKWEED BEETLE

Chrysochus cobaltinus

This insect is another one that is so darn pretty you really can't walk past it without a second glance. It looks like a great big, carefully polished, bright, shiny blue ladybug. Its body is round and plump, and its legs end in what a bugster might consider paws. In other words, it's a cute beetle and a gorgeous one as well. It is a member of the leaf beetle family, and, sure enough, it eats leaves. In particular, the Blue Milkweed Beetle eats the leaves of dogbane and milkweeds. These plants produce toxic chemicals to discourage animals from eating them, and the beetle's color is also a warning of its toxicity.

LENGTH: 0.4 in.
HABITAT: open areas.

This beetle will ooze droplets of distasteful liquid when grasped. The beetle's first line of defense, however, is the same as that of most other leaf beetles—it tucks its legs in and drops to the ground. The Blue Milkweed Beetle is closely related to the primarily eastern Dogbane Beetle (*C. auratus*), and, like its cousin, it actually prefers dogbane plants to milkweed. Both species can be found in northern California, but only around their host plants.

STUMP STABBERS
Family Ichneumonidae, Subfamily Pimplinae

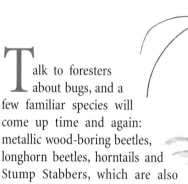

Talk to foresters about bugs, and a few familiar species will come up time and again: metallic wood-boring beetles, longhorn beetles, horntails and Stump Stabbers, which are also called "ichneumons" (pronounced "ick-NEW-monnz"). A big female Stump Stabber can be 3.3 inches long, including its immense ovipositor, and it looks like something that could definitely hurt you. In fact, many people think that Stump Stabbers sting, despite the assurances of entomologists to the contrary.

If you find a Stump Stabber, follow it. A female Stump Stabber will fly from tree trunk to tree trunk, all the while rapidly drumming her antennae as she runs around on the bark, quite obviously searching for something. Then, she stops. Somehow, she has detected a wood-boring grub, deep beneath her feet. At this point, she brings her ovipositor to bear, like some sort of strange miniature oil rig. The insect strains to work the tool into the wood, and eventually she finds the larva and forces a slender, very compressible egg down the tube and into the tunnels of her host. There, the egg hatches, and the Stump Stabber grub proceeds to find and burrow into its victim, devouring it from the inside out, leaving its essential organs to the last.

LENGTH: with ovipositor, 3.3 in or more.
HABITAT: forests.

PACIFIC CUCKOO WASP

Chrysis pacifica

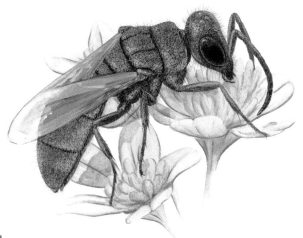

There's no crisis, it's just a *Chrysis*! The Pacific Cuckoo Wasp doesn't sting; if you grab one or otherwise threaten it, the usual response of a cuckoo wasp is to roll up into a tight little ball. These brightly colored little wasps are solitary, and they make their living by laying eggs in the nests of other sorts of solitary wasps and bees. In this regard they are like the cuckoo birds of Europe, which also lay eggs in the nests of other species (of birds, that is, not wasps and bees). Here in North America, cuckoo birds are more inclined to rear their own young, and they don't say "cuckoo" when they sing, either. For the Pacific Cuckoo Wasp, the process is simple—first the female finds the right sort of "host" bee or wasp, then it waits until the host has stocked its nest with food and laid its own egg. Then the cuckoo wasp sneaks in and lays her own egg. When the cuckoo wasp larva hatches, it eats the egg of the host and then starts eating the food provisions.

LENGTH: about 0.2 in.
HABITAT: widespread.

Some cuckoo wasp species are bright iridescent green, others are blue, and some have red or orange hues in their color pattern as well. If you can get a look at one under a microscope or a high-power magnifying glass, you will also notice that it has a deeply textured body surface. This indicates a very strong cuticle, which protects the wasp if it is discovered and attacked by its host, and it also explains why the wasp will curl up in a ball when it wants to defend itself.

GREAT GOLDEN DIGGER
Sphex ichneumoneus

Most wasps are solitary, not colonial, and among these solitary wasps, the Great Golden Digger is one of the most spectacular. The female sometimes takes nectar from flowers, but for the most part she spends her days looking for grasshoppers. With amazing agility, she will sting a 'hopper in the nerve cord and inject a paralyzing poison. The grasshopper is then immobilized, but still alive.

With immense power and determination, the wasp then carries the grasshopper back to a burrow that she prepared some time before. Most of the time, the burrow is in hard-packed ground, which must be difficult to dig in, one might think. She opens the burrow, drags the grasshopper down into the dark, and lays an egg on it. Then she comes back to the surface, and closes the entrance, sometimes smoothing it over with a pebble held in her jaws. She then goes off to look for more prey or to dig another burrow. Meanwhile, the egg hatches and the wasp grub devours the body of the zombie grasshopper. That is, unless some other insect, such as a velvet ant (p. 85) or a parasitic fly (p. 92), gets its egg into the burrow before it is closed. If that happens, the invader will kill the baby wasp and eat the grasshopper itself.

LENGTH: about 1 in.
HABITAT: open areas.

YELLOW JACKETS
Vespula spp.

I f they didn't sting so much, these wasps would be some of our most watchable bugs. They live in colonies, like Honey Bees (*Apis mellifera*), and they build huge paper nests, sometimes high in the branches of trees, sometimes in old rodent burrows in the ground.

To make paper, Yellow Jackets chew on bark or wood and mix the pulp with saliva. Then they add each mouthful to the nest to form either the six-sided cells where the larvae are reared or the multi-layered outside cover of the nest. Because each load of pulp comes from a different source, you can see a subtle pattern of gray bands in the paper of the nest. If Yellow

LENGTH: about 0.4–0.6 in.
HABITAT: widespread.

Jackets are coming to your fence or lawn furniture for pulp, you will soon notice a series of shallow grooves where they have chewed. For food, they visit flowers and catch bugs, and they are also attracted to fallen fruit and dead meat (and to picnics, which to them look like fallen fruit and dead meat).

By the time late summer rolls around, the nests are as big as basketballs, and the hornets are ready to defend them at the slightest provocation. In fall, the colony breaks down, and only the new queens survive the winter, to start new colonies in the spring. The nests don't last long once the leaves fall—birds pick them apart. Yellow Jackets, unlike Honey Bees, can sting repeat-edly, although they do eventually run out of venom, I suppose.

GOLDEN PAPER WASP

Polistes fuscatus

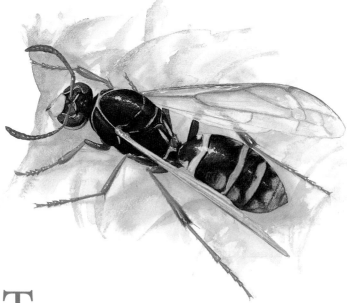

T
he name "paper wasp" really should go to Yellow Jackets (p. 83) and their relatives. By comparison, the "real" paper wasp is an amateur. Golden Paper Wasp nests are constructed beneath an overhang of some sort (often the eave of a house) and have no outside covering. The single layer of paper cells is open to the air, and these wasps never build a second or a third layer. Still, it is interesting to watch paper wasps (all the offspring of a single queen and mother) at the nest, because you can actually see what they are doing—something that can't be said of Yellow Jackets or Bald-faced Hornets (*Vespula maculata*). The colonies of Golden Paper Wasps are of moderate size, to match the moderate size of their nests. These wasps feed at flowers, especially goldenrod, and they also hunt insects for food. They have painful stings, but our local species is not a particularly defensive one, so few people get stung despite how common the wasps are.

LENGTH: about 0.7 in.
HABITAT: open areas.

To most people, this is what a "wasp" should look like: long and slender, with a tiny "waist" and narrow wings. Most newcomers to entomology are surprised to discover that thousands of other insects—many of which are tiny and compact and most of which are not even social—are also called wasps.

COW KILLERS

Dasymutilla spp.

The Cow Killers are members of a group of bugs called "velvet ants." They are not, however, ants at all. In fact, the familiar wingless, furry Cow Killers are really female wasps in the family Mutillidae. The males look more like traditional wasps, and they are smaller and less impressive than the females.

Cow Killers got their name from their sting—they have some of the most painful stings in the entire insect world. Their bright colors are a warning to potential enemies to avoid them. Cow Killers do not use their stings to kill or paralyze other bugs; instead, they look for the nests of dig-

LENGTH: about 0.6 in.
HABITAT: open, dry ground.

ging wasps and bees, and then they lay their eggs on the prey that the wasps and bees have gathered. Then the Cow Killer grub eats both the wasp grub and the paralyzed prey intended for the digger wasp.

Adult Cow Killers (and velvet ants in general) are omnivores, and they can live for many months. Because they are some of the hardiest bugs around, as well as some of the best looking, they are often exhibited in bug zoos, where they make a very interesting display.

BUMBLE BEES
Bombus spp.

Bumble Bees have a painful sting, but they are so cute and fuzzy that we love them just the same. They are slow to anger, and they are quite docile even when you are near their nest. In the spring, queens set up new colonies in the abandoned burrows of mice and voles. There, they make wax pots with open tops. Inside these pots they rear their grubs. Once the grubs grow up to be worker bees, the number of pots is increased. Some pots are used to rear the young, and others are filled with pollen or honey.

Bumble Bees visit flowers to gather both pollen and nectar. Their wings are so small for the size of their bodies that some biologists were unsure for a while about how they could possibly fly. Because they are so hairy, Bumble Bee bodies look bigger than they are. The hair helps hold body heat when they fly, and they can fly at lower temperatures than many other bees. One friend of mine claims that when the Bumble Bees come out in the spring, so do the bears, and when the bees go in for the winter, the bears do, too.

LENGTH: usually 0.4–0.8 in.
HABITAT: clearings and meadows.

CARPENTER BEES

Xylocopa spp.

Almost everyone thinks of these bees as "big, black Bumble Bees." Interestingly enough, however, they are quite different from Bumble Bees (p. 86) in many ways other than their color—which is actually iridescent blue-black and not merely black. As their name suggests, Carpenter Bees do indeed nest in wood, in burrow nests that they make themselves. Usually the wood is dead, and they will sometimes use fence posts, power poles and other sorts of lumber, including the sides of houses. The nest itself

LENGTH: up to 1 in.
HABITAT: widespread in a variety of habitats.

consists of a dead-end tunnel provisioned with food for the larvae. Each larval "cell" is separated from the next by a wall of wood chips. This nesting arrangement is common in solitary wasps and bees, and it means that the occupant of the cell closest to the exit has to emerge before the next bee, and so on. Pity the last Carpenter Bee at the end of the tunnel, patiently waiting for its siblings to get out of the way!

Adult Carpenter Bees visit flowers and take pollen and nectar. Like many other sorts of bees, Carpenters will sometimes chew through the bottom of the flower at the side rather than politely taking their meal by approaching from the center. Of course, when they take this shortcut, they do not pollinate the flower.

CARPENTER ANTS

Camponotus spp.

C arpenter Ants are
not termites (p. 114),
and termites are not "white ants."
They are both social insects, but ants
have a pupal stage, and termites do not.
Furthermore, all worker ants are adult
females, whereas worker termites come in all ages and both sexes. Carpenter
Ants are the biggest ants in our area. They move slowly, and they are not particularly aggressive. They have no sting, and, like many related sorts of ants,
their main defense is to bite. Their jaws are strong, because they chew
through wood for a living, and in that way they are similar to termites.

In the wild, you can spot a Carpenter Ant nest in a tree trunk by the pile
of sawdust outside the entrance. These ants sometimes build their homes
inside the woodwork of older houses, and there again the thing to watch for
is sawdust. They don't actually eat
the wood, but in the course of exca-
vating their galleries, they certainly
do weaken it, to the point where the
tree, or the expensive house, might "fail," as the engineers say. Woodpeckers
love to eat these ants, and it is fitting that our biggest ant is continually under
attack from our biggest woodpecker, the pileated woodpecker.

LENGTH: about 0.5 in.
HABITAT: forested areas.

GIANT CRANE FLIES

Holorusia spp.

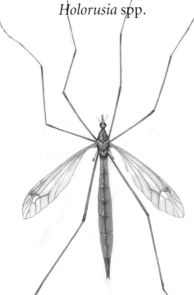

"Aaaaaaggh! A monster mosquito!" That's what most people say the first time they see a Giant Crane Fly, an event that usually occurs while the fly is resting on the side of a suburban house. There are many species of crane flies, but the giant ones are extra large, and they have menacing-looking snouts. These flies look evil, but the truth is you couldn't ask for a nicer bug: they don't bite at all, they are actually sort of attractive, and even the larvae are unobtrusive, living as scavengers in the soil and in rotting logs. The European Crane Fly (*Tipula paludosa*), however, has larvae, called "leather-jackets," that can be lawn pests in our area.

Some people call these flies "daddy long-legs," a term that is most often used to refer to Harvestmen (p. 146), which are a sort of arachnid. In general, then, we are surrounded by confusion with respect to Giant Crane Flies, and hopefully this book will help dispel our ignorance. Another frequent twist to the finding-one-in-your-garden story is the fact that they are often discovered while mating, end to end. When a mating pair is disturbed, the sight of two sets of wispy, flailing wings and 12 immense, dangling legs attached to two giant "mosquitoes" that are tugging in opposite directions makes for a spectacle that is, let's just say, "creepy," to all but the most devoted bugsters among us.

LENGTH: up to 1.4 in.
HABITAT: forested areas.

89

HORSE FLIES

Hybomitra spp. & *Tabanus* spp.

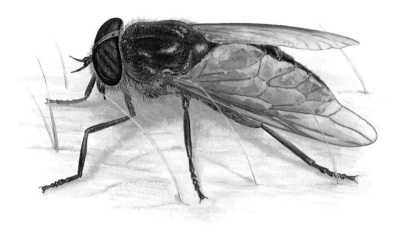

So what could be interesting about a Horse Fly? Well, how about the colors in its eyes? If you get a close-up look at one—perhaps after a lucky swat—check out the eyes and the intense rainbows that enliven its otherwise evil-looking face. These flies feed on blood, and they are most common near lakes. Go for a swim in mid-summer, and I guarantee that by the time you have dried yourself off you will have taken at least one swing at a Horse Fly. These flies are attracted to large mammals (such as ourselves), and the thing they look for is a dark object with a light spot on it where the sun forms a reflective "highlight." If you drive a black car or a black van, you will find even more of them when you get back to the parking lot.

LENGTH: about 0.6 in.
HABITAT: open areas near water.

One good thing about Horse Flies is that they are so big it's hard for one to bite without you knowing it is there. As well, Horse Flies have large blades in their mouthparts, rather than sophisticated, slender stylets like a mosquito. If you find a smaller version of a Horse Fly, with dark markings on its wings, it is probably a Deer Fly (*Chrysops* spp.). Given the chance, mind you, Horse Flies will bite deer, Deer Flies will bite horses, and either one will bite people, any chance they get.

BEEISH ROBBER FLIES

Laphria spp.

Robber flies don't really steal things, other than life itself. They are amazingly agile predators, and they catch and kill other insects in mid-air. Between hunts, they find a perch on the ground or on vegetation, and from there they scan for potential victims. Their large compound eyes give them excellent vision and an amazing ability not only to spot their prey but also to follow it through the air in high-speed pursuit. When a robber fly catches something, it returns to the ground with its fearsome proboscis deep in the tissues of its unlucky prey. Robber flies are not too distantly related to Horse Flies (p. 90), and they have roughly similar sorts of mouthparts.

Even beetles can fall prey to robber flies, and the flies have perfected a way to kill these heavily armored insects. While the beetle is flying, its wing covers are spread, exposing the soft abdomen underneath. The robber fly sinks its mouthparts into the beetle's soft spot while the two are still in the air. Most robber flies are not mimics, but the Beeish Robber Fly looks so much like a Bumble Bee (p. 86) that it is tough to tell the two apart without a close look.

> **LENGTH:** about 0.8 in.
> **HABITAT:** shrubby or forested areas.

SAND DUNE BEE FLY
Poecilanthrax willistoni

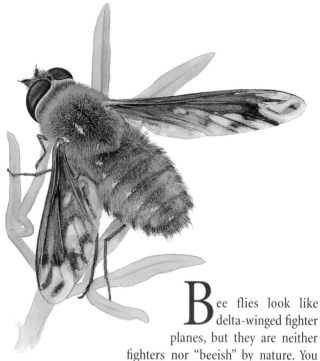

Bee flies look like delta-winged fighter planes, but they are neither fighters nor "beeish" by nature. You can generally recognize members of this family by their swept-back, dark-colored wings, but some species have clear wings, and they are easy to confuse with hover flies (p. 93). The Sand Dune Bee Fly has a distinctive pattern (see illustration) that distinguishes it from other bee flies.

The Sand Dune Bee Fly, true to its name, is found mainly on bare sand. There, it searches for certain sorts of caterpillars that serve as food for its parasitic larvae. In the same environments, other sorts of bee flies will parasitize tiger beetle (pp. 60–61) larvae or the larvae of solitary wasps (p. 82) and bees. It can be amusing to watch the flies hovering above a tiger beetle or a wasp burrow, flicking eggs into the opening. However, these flies are attracted to any roundish hole in the ground, and they will also flick eggs into the lace holes of your shoes. Not to worry—the larvae never survive in human feet, and they probably don't even make it past your socks.

LENGTH: about 0.5 in.
HABITAT: open areas, especially dry ones.

DRONE FLY
Eristalis tenax

T he Drone Fly is a sort of hover fly, but instead of mimicking wasps like most hover flies do, this species mimics the common Honey Bee (*Apis mellifera*). The Honey Bee is a fairly dull-colored insect, patterned in browns and black, a fact that seems strange in some ways, because such a hard-stinging insect might seem deserving of better warning colors.

LENGTH: about 0.6 in.
HABITAT: widespread in a variety of habitats.

Both the Honey Bee and the Drone Fly were introduced from Europe. Because the Drone Fly has larger eyes than a worker (female) Honey Bee, it was named for the Honey Bee drone (the male). The larva of the Drone Fly is the famous "Rat-tailed Maggot" that lives in the muck at the bottom of ponds and breathes through a long siphon that looks a bit like a rat's tail.

In England, many people study hover flies as a hobby, and there they enjoy the luxury of being able to buy color field guides to their local species. Perhaps some day we will reach the same level of sophistication here, but for the moment just recognizing hover flies at all is a good thing. It is also important to appreciate how many hover flies are involved in the pollination of flowers, because they visit blossoms the same way bees do.

93

ANT LIONS
Family Myrmeleontidae

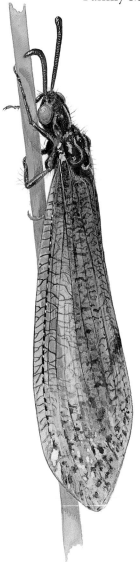

LENGTH: up to 1.4 in.
HABITAT: open, dry areas with fine sand or silt in which to dig.

At first glance, an adult Ant Lion looks much like a dull brown damselfly (pp. 116–18). Note, however, its long antennae, which are quite different from the tiny antennae of damselflies. Ant Lion adults are gentle and quite pretty in their own way. We mostly notice them as they fly to lights at night, although you may also flush them from low vegetation when you go for a walk in places where the larvae live.

Ant Lion larvae are the reason this group of bugs got its name (a literal translation of "Myrmeleontidae"). The larvae live in the sand, where they bury themselves almost completely. Then, like living land mines, they wait. Some lie just below the sand surface in flat places, but others (the more typical Ant Lions, the ones called "Doodlebugs") dig conical pits. When an ant or some other small ground-dwelling bug wanders by, the Ant Lion larva flicks sand at it. With luck, the ant will fall into the pit, where the larva grasps it with long mandibles. The mandibles are hollow, and through them the Ant Lion sucks the lifeblood of its victims.

GREEN LACEWINGS

Chrysopa spp.

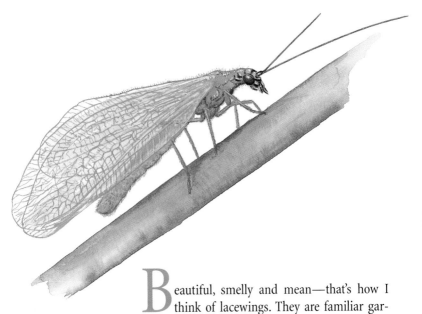

Beautiful, smelly and mean—that's how I think of lacewings. They are familiar garden bugs. The adults are truly elegant with their many-veined wings, their delicate lime-green bodies and their bulging, golden eyes. The scientific name *Chrysopa* means exactly that: "golden eyes." Catch a lacewing, however, and you will soon notice a truly weird smell as it twists and turns in your fingers as you hold it by the wings. The smell is a bit like coffee, but not really.

As for the mean-spirited aspect of their nature, lacewings are predators, and they mostly eat aphids. Thus, they join ladybugs (pp. 74–75) and the larvae of some hover flies in a "friends of the gardener" category, despite the fact that none of them even know what a gardener is. Young lacewings, which are larvae much like those of a ladybug, are also aphid eaters. They are so vicious that the mother lacewing lays each egg on the top of a long, slender stalk so the first larva to hatch doesn't eat all of its brothers and sisters before they can get out of their eggs. In addition to green lacewings, watch for brown ones and even blotchy ones (both in the family Hemerobiidae), usually early and late in the season.

> **LENGTH:** about 0.4 in.
> **HABITAT:** widespread wherever there are shrubs or forests.

SNAKEFLIES
Agulla spp.

Like the lacewings (p. 95), ant lions (p. 94) and alderflies to which they are clearly related, the Snakeflies are members of the order Neuroptera. However, some scientists place them in their own order, Raphidioptera. The clues we need to unravel these relationships are now, unfortunately, more than 300 million years old, so you'll have to forgive entomologists for their confusion on this matter.

Snakeflies have an elongated head and thorax, resulting in a front end that looks a bit like a snake's head—so long as you ignore the six legs and lacy wings that lie behind. Snakeflies prey on other small bugs, and they are often seen on flowers or other vegetation. They are truly western bugs, and in North America none are found east of the Rockies. As well, the Snakeflies in general form a group that is found mainly in the north-temperate parts of the globe, and that is almost completely absent from the tropics. As a West Coast bugster, I hope you take some pride in this nifty creature, which is often completely unfamiliar to your colleagues elsewhere.

LENGTH: about 0.5 in.
HABITAT: open, shrubby areas.

BIG GREEN STINK BUGS

Chlorochroa spp.

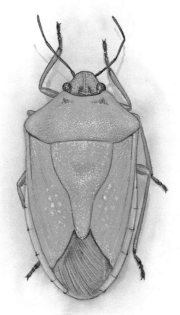

Stink bugs stink. They do so with scent glands that produce a chemical with an odor unlike anything else that you or I are likely to ever encounter. The odor makes them easy to recognize up close, but they are also obvious in other ways. Stink bugs have broad, pointed shoulders and a large, triangular plate in the middle of their back (the scutellum, for those

LENGTH: about 0.5 in.
HABITAT: shrubby and grassy areas, sometimes cropland.

who like to know these things). Some stink bugs are more triangular than others, so if in doubt, sniff. The Say's Stink Bug (*C. sayi*) is one of our biggest Big Green Stink Bugs, and it is a lovely green color.

Some stink bugs feed on other insects, but the Big Green Stink Bugs suck the juices from plants and plant seeds. Stink bugs are known not only for their odor, but also for their maternal devotion. The mother will lay a cluster of intricately sculptured eggs all together on the surface of a leaf. Then she will guard the brood until they hatch, at which point the babies are free to fend for themselves. Baby stink bugs, like all sucking bugs, are much like tiny adults, but without wings. They do, however, stink, right from their earliest days.

97

ROUGH STINK BUGS

Brochymena spp.

T he Rough Stink Bugs are among our most abundant kinds of stink bugs (family Pentatomidae), and it is a shame that they are not particularly colorful. These predators are often found under the bark of dead trees in winter and on top of the bark in spring.

It is interesting to compare the Rough Stink Bugs with the Harlequin Bug (p. 99). Both kinds of insects are stink bugs, and both produce defensive chemicals. Thus, both use their stinkiness to deter birds and other predators from eating them. Yet Rough Stink Bugs are camouflaged in color, like tree bark, whereas Harlequin Bugs are brightly colored as a warning, making them super-easy to spot. This is a very good example of how the evolutionary process comes up with multiple different "solutions" to the same "problem" (the problem of how to be a successful stink bug). When you read statements like "this species tastes bad, and therefore it is brightly colored," take them with a grain of salt. And yes, I know that I have written many sentences of this sort myself, and there are indeed a few in this very book. Just remember that bad-tasting chemicals do not necessarily lead to bright colors and vice versa.

LENGTH: 0.5 in.
HABITAT: widespread in forests.

HARLEQUIN BUG

Murgantia histrionica

I find animal names amusing. The Harlequin Bug is a type of stink bug. "Harlequin" refers to a character in pantomime with a colorful, diamond-patterned costume, vaguely like the pattern on this bug's back. Of course, Harlequin is also a brand of romance novel, widely considered cheesy, but fiercely defended by its fans. In a semi-related way, the specific epithet (the second part of the scientific name) *histrionica* is a reference to over-the-top theatrics, and if you like birds you may have noticed that

LENGTH: about 0.4 in.
HABITAT: weedy places and gardens.

the Harlequin Duck's scientific name is *Histrionicus histrionicus*. Or perhaps you didn't—too many people ignore scientific names. *Murgantia* is more of a mystery to me, but I suspect it means "beautiful mouse."

Of course, these names tell us much more about the inner workings of biologists' minds than about the animals themselves. To watch Harlequin Bugs, you'd never think they were theatrical at all. They feed on the juices of plants, especially those in the mustard family, and their bright colors are a warning to birds that, like all stink bugs, they stink. Harlequin Bugs are most abundant in warmer areas at lower elevations.

AMBUSH BUG
Phymata pacifica

Small but dangerous, that's an Ambush Bug. Ambush Bugs aren't dangerous to people, mind you, but to any sort of insect that visits flowers, they are "trouble in the raw." In the same fashion as a Goldenrod Flower Spider (p. 149), they lie in wait for the unwary pollinators, sometimes tucking in deep among the flower parts so that they stay well hidden. Our Ambush Bug is a yellowish color, and it has large, angular flanges on the sides of its abdomen. Perhaps these flanges help break up its outline and enhance the ambush effect.

An Ambush Bug has strong middle and hind legs that it uses to hold tight to a flower. Its front legs in particular are enormously strong for their size; with these clutches the Ambush Bug can subdue even a gigantic Bumble Bee (p. 86) or a butterfly many times its own size. Then, in typical predatory bug fashion, it injects a digestive fluid into its prey, waits for the insides of the insect to soften and then sucks the insides from its victim. I have seen these insects mainly in the latter part of the summer, when they are easiest to find among the flowers of goldenrod and rabbit-brush plants.

LENGTH: about 0.4 in.
HABITAT: open areas.

WESTERN BOXELDER BUG

Boisea rubrolineatus

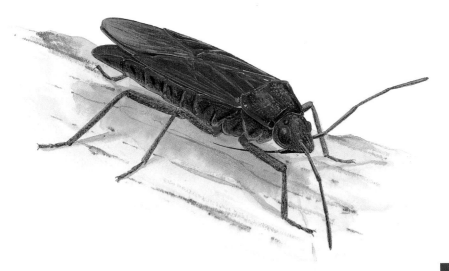

I n some places, this insect is referred to as the "Maple Bug," and people who have never heard it referred to by its official common name often "correct" my identification of this species and its relatives. It is true that these bugs feed mainly on the seeds of the maple trees. In fact, the name "boxelder" comes from an alternative common name for the ash-leaf maple, *Acer negundo*.

Most people don't like Western Boxelder Bugs, because they have a habit of congregating in houses to spend the winter. After all, when the family is gathering around the table for New Year's dinner, and a big, clumsy Boxelder Bug goes buzzing across the room, bangs into the chandelier and lands in the mashed potatoes, who can blame anyone for taking offense? It is

LENGTH: about 0.5 in.
HABITAT: widespread in a variety of habitats.

important at moments like this to remember that these bugs don't do any harm, and that up close they are actually quite handsome. Bugsters will immediately recognize the function of their black and red colors—to warn predators that they taste bad (even though they don't smell bad). When they are young, they are even more colorful, more red than black. It is only when they get their wings, as adults, that the mainly black wings cover the bright red abdomen.

CICADAS
Family Cicadidae

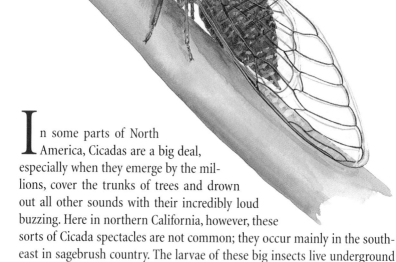

I n some parts of North America, Cicadas are a big deal, especially when they emerge by the millions, cover the trunks of trees and drown out all other sounds with their incredibly loud buzzing. Here in northern California, however, these sorts of Cicada spectacles are not common; they occur mainly in the southeast in sagebrush country. The larvae of these big insects live underground for years, feeding on roots, before emerging early one summer. To find a Cicada, you first have to learn what it sounds like: a prolonged dry, rattling buzz or a shrill whine. That's the male, and he sits on a slender branch while singing, often three or more yards above the ground. If you are very stealthy, you may be able to get close enough to spot him. One false move, however, and he will either fly away or go silent.

The sound is produced by a vibrating mechanism in the abdomen, a resonating chamber and a thin membrane something like a banjo skin. For their size, these insects can be incredibly noisy. Cicadas are another sort of bug with a built-in argument, with some people saying "SICK-uh-DAHH" or "sih-KAH-duh" and others insisting on "sick-AY-dah." All are correct, of course, but I'll let you in on the fact that most entomologists I know say "sick-AY-dah." Many people call these bugs "locusts," but this name is best reserved for certain sorts of grasshoppers (p. 104).

LENGTH: most are about 0.8 in.
HABITAT: dry, forested or shrubby areas.

ROCK CRAWLERS
Family Grylloblattidae

To find these amazing wingless insects, either one has to venture high into the mountains and search among the talus slopes and lava fields, or one must descend into the moist coastal forests and search among the soft, mossy undergrowth. In addition, some species of Rock Crawlers live in caves. The order to which these insects belong was one of the latest to be discovered by science. In 1914, Edmund Walker became the first scientist to describe Rock Crawlers; his specimens came from Banff National Park in Alberta, Canada. He realized that he was looking at not only a new species, but also a new genus, a new family and a new order—in other words a whole new kind of a bug!

To entomologists, Rock Crawlers are interesting because they are so "primitive looking." That means they look like "average" bugs from which a lot of others could have evolved. To ordinary folks, they have other interesting attributes. For example, if you pick up a Rock Crawler and hold it in your hand, the heat from your hulking mammalian body will kill it.

LENGTH: up to 1.2 in.
HABITAT: cool alpine or forested areas, lava fields and caves.

That's how well adapted these bugs are to cool climates. Adult Rock Crawlers are likely to live to be seven years old, by the way, and they feed mainly on other insects, especially wingless crane flies.

ROAD DUSTER

Dissosteira carolina

This big grasshopper is typically the one that inhabits vacant lots, construction sites, railroad tracks and gravel pits. It is often called the "Carolina Locust" or "Carolina Grasshopper." With its black hind wings, which have a narrow, white border, this remarkable 'hopper in flight looks like a Mourning Cloak butterfly (p. 39). As a young bug fanatic, I was fooled more than once by this resemblance. Recently, some entomologists have suggested that various band-winged grasshoppers (the subgroup to which the Road Duster belongs) resemble certain butterflies for a reason. The patterns on some butterflies may advertise to birds that the butterfly is a super-fast flyer, not worth pursuing, and a similar-looking grasshopper would likewise be ignored. (Other band-winged grasshoppers, which resemble sulphur butterflies, are believed to benefit from similar mimicry.) The Road Duster's main defense when in flight, however, is to simply drop to the ground and fold its wings. While on the ground, it is extremely difficult to see because of its cinnamon-brown-and-gray body. It resembles a dirt lump—even its eyes are a mottled, dusty color.

LENGTH: 1.2–1.6 in.
HABITAT: open, dry places.

Males do an interesting courtship display, the hover flight: watch for a male to hover in mid-air, about three feet above the ground, fluttering its wings softly, first quickly and then at a lower speed.

ANGULAR-WINGED KATYDID

Microcentrum rhombifolium

atydids are wonderful plant mimics. They move slowly, on long, thin legs, and their wings and bodies really do look like green leaves. In the tropics, many katydids are even more leaf-like than ours, with fake bite marks in their wings or fake mold patches. Disguised among the leaves of the trees and shrubs in which they live, katydids carry out their leaf-eating lives. The males chirp to attract the females, and it is from the sound that

LENGTH: about 2.4 in.
HABITAT: open areas.

one species makes that the name "katy-did" was derived, or at least that's what we think happened. The katydids belong to a number of subgroups within a larger group of grigs called "long-horned grasshoppers." Indeed, katydids have long antennae, but some members of this gang are wingless, making them much less like a classic katydid than others.

The Angular-winged Katydid (or Broad-winged Katydid, as it is sometimes called) is one of many katydid species in northern California. Formerly restricted to eastern North America, it has only recently colonized the West Coast.

FIELD CRICKETS

Gryllus spp.

There is no more classic sound of summer than the chirping of crickets. Seeing one chirp, on the other hand, is no easy matter. If you do manage to get a peek, you'll find that it is only the males that make sounds. Males have two pointy things (the cerci) sticking out the back of the abdomen, whereas females have three (two cerci and one egg-laying ovipositor). To make the sound, and hopefully attract females, male crickets rub their two wing covers together, bringing a rasp into contact with a file. The hardened wing covers amplify and resonate to produce the noise we all know and love.

Field Crickets rarely venture into houses. The familiar cricket of the hearth is the House Cricket (*Acheta domestica*) of Europe. The House Cricket is brown, whereas the Field Cricket is black. These days, the House Cricket is actually big bug business, because many cricket farms now supply them to pet stores as food for captive frogs, lizards, tarantulas and fishes. The House Cricket is generally unable to live outdoors all year in our area, although there are a few such colonies in the warmer parts of California.

LENGTH: about 0.8 in.
HABITAT: open areas.

CAVE CRICKETS
Ceuthophilus spp.

The Cave Crickets, in some places, actually live in caves. Here, however, they mostly live in rodent burrows, under rocks and logs, and in rotten wood. What they want is a place that is moist and dark. For those people who think *Homo sapiens* has advanced beyond the "caveman" stage, all I can say is—look in your basement. There, on occasion, you will indeed find a Cave Cricket or two. They need access to water, and they are therefore usually found somewhere near the floor drain. Don't let them worry you, however, because they do no harm. Some people mistake them for cockroaches (p. 115), but I'm assuming that if you are reading this book, you won't do that.

Another name for *Ceuthophilus* Cave Crickets is "Camel Crickets," based on their hump-backed shape. Note as well that they have no wings, and therefore they cannot chirp like other crickets. Ours have very long antennae, but the true cave dwellers (in our area, *Tropidischia xanthostoma*) have even longer feelers, as well as elongate legs. There is a painting of a Cave Cricket

LENGTH: about 0.5 in.
HABITAT: widespread.

in among the famous cave paintings of France, some 16,000 years old. It is the oldest depiction of an insect that has ever been discovered. And as they say in France, *plus ça change, plus c'est la même chose*—the more things change, the more they stay the same!

JERUSALEM CRICKET

Stenopelmatus fuscus

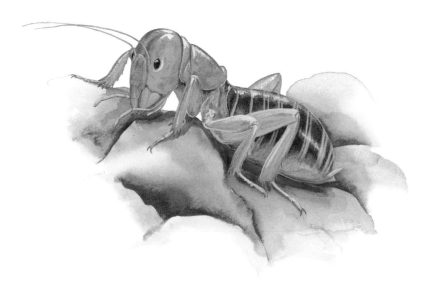

The Jerusalem Cricket is a big-headed, slow-moving creature that lives in a variety of habitats in this area, including gardens. It is an opportunist and a scavenger that will eat any sort of plant or animal material that it finds in its nocturnal wanderings. Some people call it the "Potato Bug," because it will feed on potatoes given half a chance.

If you want to see this bug, you might try an old night-bugging trick that I learned from entomologists in Arizona. When you first start out at night with your flashlight, take a few moments and place little piles of dry, uncooked oatmeal here and there. Supposedly, Jerusalem Crickets love oatmeal, and they will slowly make their way toward the pile. Then, when you are packing up and getting ready for the drive home, long after midnight, you check the oatmeal. I've been told that you can sometimes find dozens of Jerusalem Crickets this way, but so far all I have seen is ants. The easiest way to find Jerusalem Crickets is to flip rocks and boards over during the day.

LENGTH: up to 2 in.
HABITAT: widespread and common.

CALIFORNIA WALKINGSTICKS

Timema spp.

I f you watch nature television or visit bug zoos, you probably have a mental image of a typical walkingstick—a long, thin insect with long, thin legs. But just as all sticks are not shaped alike, neither are the bugs that imitate them. The California Walkingsticks are relatively short-legged and wide-bodied. As well, they have a back-up plan if their stick-like camouflage fails them—they run like the wind and puff bad-smelling chemicals into the faces of their predators. They are found mostly early in the season, and, although most are green, some are brown or pink. Seriously—pink! Who ever heard of a pink stick?

LENGTH: 1.4 in.
HABITAT: chapparal and oak woodland.

One way to find these well-concealed creatures is to spread a sheet under a shrub or tree and then firmly but respectfully beat the branches with a stick. The walkingsticks should fall onto the sheet, along with spiders, ladybugs and many other fascinating insects. This is often a good way to locate hornet nests as well, so don't say you weren't forewarned...

NARROW-WINGED MANTID
Tenodera angustipennis

Praying mantids (or mantises, if you prefer) are well-known insects. You sometimes see Narrow-winged Mantids and Chinese Mantids (*T. aridifolia*) offered for sale in garden shops for control of pests in gardens. Neither is native to this area. They also could care less about pest control, but let's not hold that against them. I sometimes buy mantid egg cases, because I find it fascinating to watch them hatch and to rear the baby mantids. Hundreds come from a single egg mass, and the babies are almost instantly cannibalistic. Unless you separate them, you will soon have only one mantid! Mantids grow slowly, over the course of the summer, and it is easy to get them to take bugs from your fingers and to sit on your hand while they eat.

Because mantids can turn their heads and look at whatever interests them, they have a wonderfully humanoid look. Their upright posture and grasping forelegs add to the effect. Another introduced species, the European Mantid (*Mantis religiosa*) is found fairly regularly in northern California's warmer areas. It is the species that led to the name "praying mantis"; entomologists were inspired by the way it holds its forelegs as if in prayer. The name "mantis" also has a religious meaning: it is a Greek word that refers to prophets. The scientific equivalent, "mantid," is the short form of the family name, Mantidae.

LENGTH: about 2.8–3.9 in.
HABITAT: gardens and shrubby areas.

MINOR GROUND MANTID

Litaneutria minor

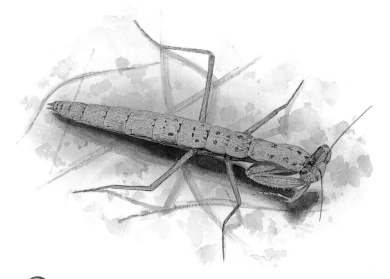

Our smallest native mantid is the Minor Ground Mantid, and it is certainly an interesting one. The Minor Ground Mantid lives on the ground or in low vegetation. The females are wingless, but the males have wings. Gray-brown in color, they are active both day and night. Among the North American mantids, of which there are 18 species, this one is a bit of an oddball (because it lives on the ground and because of its size), but it is not the only small one. Most mantids live in leafy vegetation, but some prefer tree trunks, flowers or, like the Minor Ground Mantid, open ground. It is in

LENGTH: about 1.2 in.
HABITAT: dry, open areas.

the tropics that mantids reach their greatest diversity, and if you think North American mantids are nifty, you should see some of the flower-mimicking and lichen-like mantids from Africa and Asia or the great big banjo-shaped mantids from Central America that look like fallen seed pods.

Like all other mantids, the Minor Ground Mantid can turn its head to look in any direction it pleases, and it is a lightning-fast predator, catching other bugs with its spiked forelegs. And yes, on occasion, a female will eat her mate during the act of copulation, and he will, indeed, continue mating, even without his brain. Apart from this last unfortunate feature, mantids are surely the most human-like of all bugs.

CALIFORNIA MANTID
Stagmomantis californica

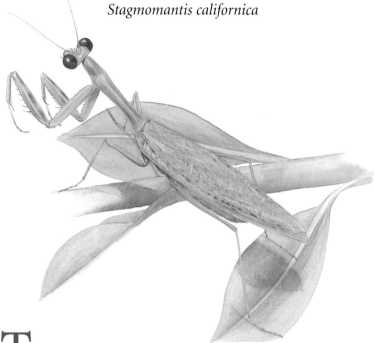

T he California Mantid is another native species, as its name so appropriately suggests. It is perhaps not as well known as its close eastern relative, the Carolina Mantid (*S. carolina*), but the two species are alike in most respects, though the Carolina is slightly smaller. In fact, there are a few records of the Carolina Mantid in California, so you might encounter both species if you look hard enough.

The California Mantid is medium sized, as mantids go, and it comes in three different colors: green, yellow and brown. It is not uncommon to find this sort of "color polymorphism" in insects that have camouflage colors for hiding in vegetation, and presumably all three colors work well at one time or another, depending on the habitat and the time of year. The female

LENGTH: about 2.4 in.
HABITAT: dry, shrubby areas in the Sacramento Valley.

California Mantid has short wings that do not cover the entire abdomen, and, like many other female mantids, she cannot fly. Once the female is full of developing eggs, she is too heavy to fly anyway, so why should she bother with long wings? The male, on the other hand, is a good flier, with wings that cover his entire abdomen throughout his life.

EUROPEAN EARWIG

Forficula auricularia

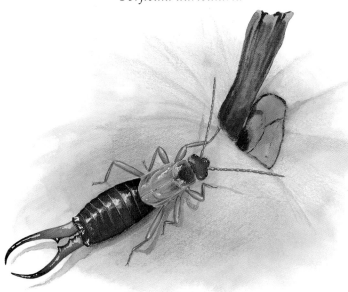

Very few insects generate the confusion that earwigs do. For reasons that have never been clear, people often believe that they drill into human ears, that they are filthy, and that they can pinch very hard with their cerci. But, according to entomologists, who should know, they don't do any of these things. As for how earwigs got their name, your guess is as good as mine. The European Earwig is an introduced species, originally native to Europe, which arrived in North America around 1919. Thus, the name "earwig" is not of local origin.

The truth is that earwigs are interesting, mostly harmless creatures. They are also good parents who guard their eggs and newborn young. Some species of earwigs are parasitic on other sorts of bugs, whereas others are omnivores, predators, scavengers or plant feeders. It is the plant-feeding ones, which include the European Earwig, that we see most often. The European Earwig will readily feed on flowers, vegetables and fruits, which naturally angers the gardener who grew them. Here is one species that even a bugster would have trouble defending.

LENGTH: about 0.5 in.
HABITAT: gardens and open areas.

GIANT DAMPWOOD TERMITES

Zootermopsis spp.

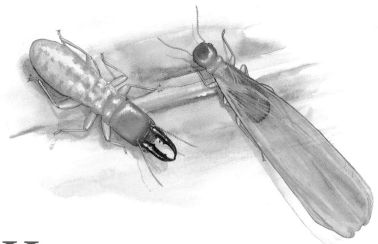

How lucky can you get—some of the biggest termites on earth live right here in northern California. Termites are social insects, but, unlike ants, bees and wasps, they do not go through a pupal stage. So, young termites, which serve as workers for the colony, look much like the adults. And, again unlike ants, bees and wasps, whose workers are all female, termites form colonies made up of both males and females. When they mature, termites can be workers, soldiers or winged "reproductives." Giant Dampwood Termite workers are about 0.4 inches long, but a big soldier can be up to 1 inch long, with strong jaws—a very impressive bug.

LENGTH: soldiers up to 1 in.
HABITAT: coastal forests.

However, unless you dig into rotting logs, the termites you are most likely to encounter are the winged ones. They can be seen on their late-summer flights as they look for mates and attempt to start new colonies. Once the queen settles into the job of egg laying, she becomes bloated and helpless; she is cared for by workers throughout her 20 or more years of life.

Termites eat wood, as anyone knows who lives in a wooden house, but they can't do it without some help. Approximately one-third of a termite's body weight is made up of microscopic protozoans. These "gut symbionts" digest the cellulose in the wood.

GERMAN COCKROACH
Blatella germanica

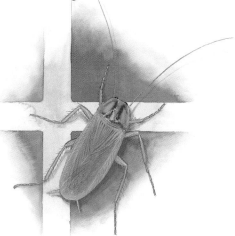

I t is unfortunate for the German people that this cockroach is named in their country's honor. It is also unfortunate for the many thousands of harmless woodland cockroaches that live in the tropics around the world that we temperate folks get such a poor introduction to the order's diversity and splendor. Of course, most of the cockroaches we find in this part of the world are introduced species, and all of these introduced roaches are capable of "infesting" houses and other buildings. We can take pride, however, in a native species of large Colonial Wood Roach (*Cryptocercus punctulatus*), as well as the Western Wood Cockroach (*Parcoblatta americana*) and a few species of dryland roaches in the genera *Eremoblatta* and *Arenivaga*.

German Cockroaches especially seem to like greenhouses, kitchens and bathrooms. Once under a safe roof, they feed on just about anything edible, although they do need water, which they get from condensation or from water traps and drainpipes. They are active after dark, and they

LENGTH: about 0.6 in.
HABITAT: buildings, potentially anywhere in our area.

are very difficult to catch. Their cerci (the two feelers on the end of the abdomen) can detect even the slightest breezes, and cockroaches instantly run when they feel the pressure wave of an approaching foot. Cockroaches are very rarely implicated in the spread of disease, despite what you might hear. Generally, they are most abundant in places where things are most messy, and in those sorts of environments diseases have no problem getting around by themselves.

BOREAL BLUET

Enallagma boreale

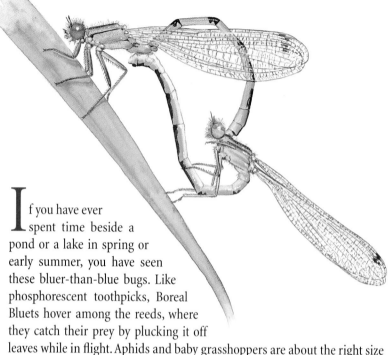

I f you have ever spent time beside a pond or a lake in spring or early summer, you have seen these bluer-than-blue bugs. Like phosphorescent toothpicks, Boreal Bluets hover among the reeds, where they catch their prey by plucking it off leaves while in flight. Aphids and baby grasshoppers are about the right size for a damselfly to tackle, and yes, the Boreal Bluet is a type of damselfly. More specifically, it is a type of American bluet.

The males are patterned in blue and black, but some females are green or yellow instead of blue. To be honest, our five species of American bluets all look more or less exactly alike. In cases like this, entomology books usu-

LENGTH: about 1.2 in.
HABITAT: ponds and lakes.

ally say something like "identification is best left to specialists." In reality, it's not that hard—all you need is a good magnifying glass and some obscure information. More and more, however, the popularity of damselfly- and dragonfly-watching is catching up to butterfly-watching, which in turn is slowly catching up to bird-watching. If you've tried bird-watching, and if you believe that mere mortals can actually identify sparrows and shorebirds in the field, then you may some day agree that the bluets are manageable, too.

116

VIVID DANCER

Argia vivida

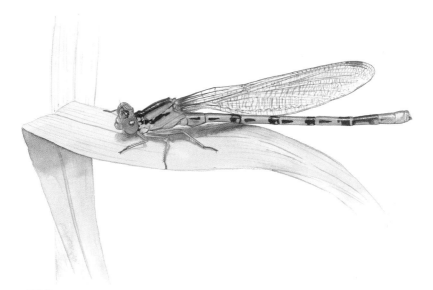

Dancers are in most respects like bluets, and both are subgroups of the damselfly clan. To the experienced eye, however, the dancers provide a glimpse of the tropics, whereas the bluets (p. 116) are more typical of temperate climes. The Vivid Dancer is a fairly typical member of its group, with lovely colors and a slightly more complex set of dark markings than you see on your average bluet. If you watch a dancer for a while, you will also notice that it is a more energetic, frenetic sort of bug: it moves in a quick, jerky fashion, and it often flicks its wings up and down rapidly, as if ready to fly

LENGTH: about 1.4 in.
HABITAT: near warm springs.

in an instant. The dancer group is represented by 10 species in California, and it is much more diverse in the tropics of Central and South America, where there are over 100 additional species.

The Vivid Dancer is interesting not only for its colors and behavior, but for its habitat as well. It will breed only in springs, and warm springs are much to its liking—the larvae of this species can tolerate water much warmer than most other damselflies would prefer, and they stay warm all winter as well. The timing of their transformation to an adult damselfly is therefore based on day length, not the temperature of the water.

CALIFORNIA SPREADWING
Archilestes californica

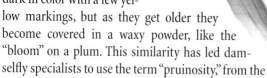

The California Spreadwing is a damselfly, and though it is less colorful than many of its relatives are, it still commands attention. When these damselflies are newly emerged adults, they are dark in color with a few yellow markings, but as they get older they become covered in a waxy powder, like the "bloom" on a plum. This similarity has led damselfly specialists to use the term "pruinosity," from the same root as "prune." Some damselflies become pruinose with age, as do some dragonflies, whereas others do not. Why the difference, no one knows for sure, but it seems likely that the pruinose markings are highly reflective ultraviolet signals that are used in courtship.

Together, damselflies and dragonflies form the insect order Odonata, and unfortunately we have no English term that refers to them both together. British people use the word "dragonfly" to include damselflies, but it seems to me that giving "dragonfly" two confusingly similar meanings is a bad idea. I prefer the term "odonates," or just simply "odes," myself. Distinguishing damselflies from dragonflies is easy: damselflies are thin, and all of their wings are similar in shape; dragonflies are more heavily built, and the hind wings are broader than the front ones. Some people will tell you that damselflies always fold their wings over their backs when they perch, but obviously the spreadwings are an exception to this rule.

LENGTH: usually 2–2.2 in.
HABITAT: near slow-flowing streams.

BLUE-EYED DARNER
Aeshna multicolor

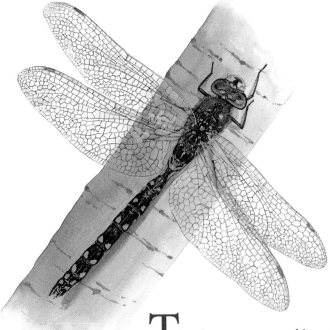

The darners are our biggest dragonflies, and the Blue-eyed Darner is one of the most common darners. Up close, the male is dark brown, patterned in blue and green, usually with beautiful blue-green, black-spotted eyes. Some of the females are also colored this way, but others are brown and yellow. Darners spend most of the day in the air cruising the mid-summer skies for insects, which they capture in flight with their long, spiny legs. Darners breed in ponds and lakes, but they will also wander far from water to feed.

The name "darner," by the way, comes from the mistaken notion that these dragonflies will sew up your lips with their stingers. In reality, they have no stingers, and they don't sew, so put aside your fears. Some entomologists have suggested that this rumor got started when people wad-

LENGTH: 2.8 in.
HABITAT: widespread.

ing in the shallows were accidentally jabbed by female darners that were trying to lay eggs. I guess a bare leg is easy to mistake for a soft water plant. Darners are on the wing from late spring all the way to late fall.

119

GREEN DARNER

Anax junius

The Green Darner is not only big and beautiful, it is also of interest because it is a migrant. Each spring, Green Darners move northward with the warm weather, usually ensuring that they are the first large dragonflies to appear on the wing in any given location. They then breed in ponds and shallow lakes, and their progeny apparently hatch out before fall and stage a return migration south. Perhaps it is this migrating tendency that has made the Green Darner the most common and widespread large dragonfly in North America. This species is also found in Hawai'i, alongside its gigantic relative the Hawai'ian Darner (*A. strenuus*).

LENGTH: up to 3.1 in.
HABITAT: near ponds and lakes.

The Male Green Darner is actually green only on the thorax—the abdomen is bright blue. In fact, the blue base of the male's abdomen is a good field mark, making this species easily recognizable at a distance. The female, on the other hand, is much more greenish looking, although her abdomen is actually grayish or brownish.

FLAME SKIMMER

Libellula saturata

The Flame Skimmer is a bright red dragonfly with loads of personality. Males are a bit redder than the orange-red females, as is the case among most red-colored dragonflies. However, few species match the Flame Skimmer for the amount of red on the body, wings and legs. Only the eyes are brownish on this spectacular dragonfly.

The Flame Skimmer is primarily a desert species, and its range extends northward only to Oregon. In the northern parts of its range, this dragonfly is found primarily in and around warm springs, where its larvae find the warmth they need. In northern California, it is found in similar habitats as well as in the warmer lowlands. Flame Skimmers are also found throughout the Southwest, where the larvae are accustomed to warm waters in places such as desert pools and other sun-warmed habitats. The adults cruise the margins of stagnant and slow-flowing waters.

> **LENGTH:** about 2.2 in.
> **HABITAT:** warm pools, slow streams and warm springs.

COMMON WHITETAIL
Libellula lydia

To my eye, the Common Whitetail is one of the prettiest of all dragonflies. I love to see it patrolling around a small pond, stopping to perch
on a low stick here or there that is just barely protruding from the water. The
broad, bright bluish-white abdomen of a mature male is a wonderfully obvious example of signal coloration. The male uses this beacon both to ward off
other males and to advertise to females. The color of the abdomen comes
from—you guessed it—pruinosity, just as in the California Spreadwing
(p. 118). Then there are the black-banded wings, contrasting dramatically
with the blue-white abdomen. You
might think that this sort of color
scheme would make the Common
Whitetail easy prey for birds, but the
truth is that few birds can outmaneuver one of these agile dragonflies in
the air. With its stout thorax, short wings and broad body, the Common
Whitetail is maneuverable indeed, as you will surely learn if you ever try to
net one.

LENGTH: about 1.8 in.
HABITAT: near ponds.

Not as colorful as her mate, the female Common Whitetail has a brown
abdomen with white flecks along the sides, and her wings each have three
black bands.

VARIEGATED MEADOWHAWK

Sympetrum corruptum

V ariegated is a word that means "marked with irregular patches of different colors," but why *corruptum*, which simply means "corrupt"? Some experts think the name must refer to the stagnant waters that are sometimes the breeding places for this species of dragonfly. When you are up to your armpits in waders trying to catch dragonflies, it's easy to form strong opinions about smelly habitats.

Like the Green Darner (p. 120), the Variegated Meadowhawk stages mass migrations, though not as regularly. It is a widespread species, but the migrations are often most noticeable right here on the West Coast. The migrations occur in fall, and they seem to be triggered by an east wind. At least, that's when observers have reported seeing huge waves of Variegated Meadowhawks moving southward along the coastline. Where they came from, and where they are going, no one yet knows! Most of these migrators are young adults, by the way, and they are less red than the mature male pictured here.

LENGTH: about 1.6 in.
HABITAT: usually near ponds and lakes.

STREAM SKATER

Aquarius remigis

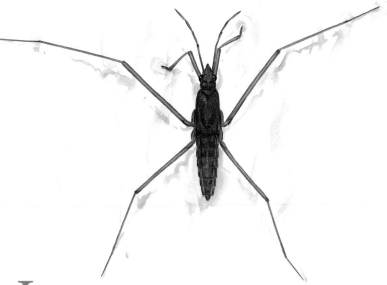

Let's face it—it's just plain weird that an animal can live on top of the water without falling through. A Stream Skater (a type of water strider) achieves this feat in a fascinating way: four very long legs support its slender body, and thus its wispy mass is distributed over a large area of the water's surface. The water itself has a sort of skin to it (the "surface tension") that is strong enough to support an insect, but only if its legs repel water, which naturally a Stream Skater's do. For these little bugs, the surface of a stream must feel like a great, slippery waterbed mattress that stretches off in all directions. On this bizarre playing-field they search for food in the form of other bugs that have fallen in and drowned or that are in the process of drowning.

Because the Stream Skater is a sucking bug, it has a piercing proboscis that allows it to overpower and consume its prey. Some full-grown Stream Skaters have wings, but others are wingless. Winged Stream Skaters can leave their home stream and settle elsewhere, but those that are wingless must be satisfied with their humble home and trust that things will remain to their liking.

LENGTH: up to 0.8 in.
HABITAT: streams and small rivers.

124

GIANT WATER BUGS

Lethocerus spp.

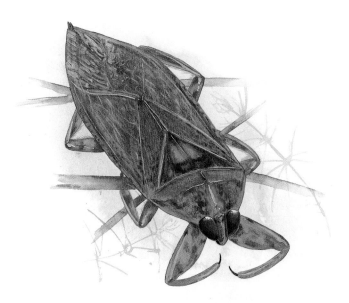

With their swollen front legs, these critters look a bit like a weightlifter holding two long spikes above his head. Oddly enough, they also look like domino-sized pieces of wet, brown cardboard. In flight, they look a lot like small bats, and they are often attracted to lights at night.

Once a Giant Water Bug grasps a luckless fish, tadpole or fellow insect, the result is inevitable. The sucking beak plunges deep, and digestive juices are injected. These juices dissolve the prey inside its own body; meanwhile, the willow-leaf–sized insect holds on and waits until the time is right to suck. When the meal is done, the bug swims off to digest, using two pairs of swimming legs rather than one. After all, these bugs are our largest aquatic insects, and they need the extra power to propel their hefty bodies through the water. Young Giant Water Bugs look much like the adults, but without wings. These impressive creatures can be found in still or slow-flowing waters, and they are most abundant in cattail marshes. And yes, if one bites you, it really does hurt.

LENGTH: 2 in.
HABITAT: ponds and lakes.

TOE BITER
Abedus indentatus

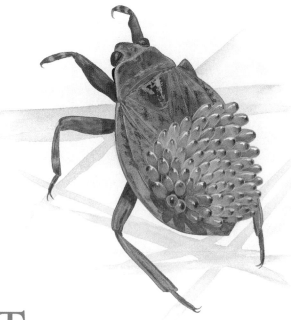

The Toe Biter is a member of the giant water bug family, but it is not quite as gigantic as its relatives in the genus *Lethocerus* (p. 125). The most interesting thing about Toe Biters, from an entomological standpoint, is how they take care of their eggs. Males and females mate in the usual fashion, but instead of laying her eggs on water plants the way other water bugs generally do, the female lays them on the back of the male. The eggs are attached with a sort of glue, and the egg mass covers most of his wings, gluing them shut and ensuring that he will not leave the pond until they hatch. It is likely that the eggs are safer on his back than they would be elsewhere, because the male can defend them from predators. As well, it is likely that the eggs are kept cleaner and get more oxygen while riding along on top of their father's back. When the eggs hatch, the young larvae simply swim away, and the father Toe Biter's responsibilities end. If you watch this process in an aquarium, however, you will soon discover that Toe Biters are not above a bit of cannibalism here and there.

LENGTH: about 1.2 in.
HABITAT: streams more often than ponds.

WATER BOATMEN
Family Corixidae

Although they are small, the Water Boatmen are amazing. Take a look at a Water Boatman's legs. The first pair are shaped like little garden trowels, and the bug uses them for sifting through muck for food. The next pair are long and pointed, and the boatman uses them to hold onto plants or rocks while underwater. Then, there are the back legs, which are the boatman's oars.

If you keep a Water Boatman in an aquarium, you can see how it breathes underwater. A layer of air clings to the boatman's tummy, and it breathes from this bubble. The oxygen the bug needs enters the bubble from the surrounding water. At the same time, carbon dioxide leaves the bubble and goes into the pond. Slowly, the bubble gets smaller as nitrogen goes into the water, and then the bug pops to the surface to replenish its air supply.

Water Boatmen live in ponds, rivers, lakes and even saline sloughs.

LENGTH: 0.2–0.4 in.
HABITAT: ponds, lakes, rivers and streams.

At times, there can be millions of them in one place, and when they mistakenly fly to lights at night and fall down disoriented, they can cover the ground with their bodies.

SINGLE-BANDED BACKSWIMMER

Notonecta unifasciata

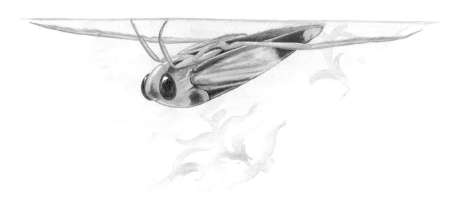

Are you any good at the backstroke? Well, it seems that the Single-Banded Backswimmer doesn't know any other way to swim. At first, you might think that a backswimmer is just an upside-down Water Boatman (p. 127), but have another look. Both pairs of front legs are short and stocky, for grabbing prey. Instead of resting on underwater plants, backswimmers lounge right at the top of the pond. They rest with their legs touching the underside of the water surface and their heads aimed slightly downward, ready to dive.

If you catch a backswimmer and flip it over, you'll see how pretty it is, with bright white wings and fiery red eyes. Don't let it bite you, though! The bite of a backswimmer is like that of a Giant Water Bug (p. 125)—intended to dissolve your flesh!

People who keep fish in outdoor ponds dread backswimmers, because they eat a lot of small fishes, as well as other bugs. In nature, however, backswimmers are both the predator and the prey, and they make the world of the pond more interesting, albeit a bit more dangerous. Backswimmers may be predators, but they themselves live in fear of such things as Giant Water Bugs, Giant Diving Beetles (p. 131) and larger fishes.

LENGTH: 0.4 in.
HABITAT: ponds, lakes and slow streams.

WATER SCORPIONS

Ranatra spp.

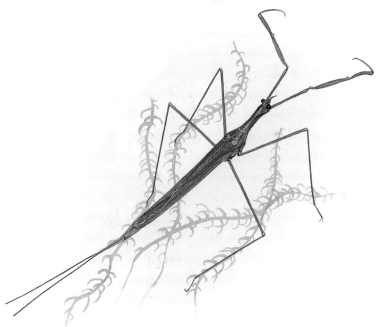

Structurally, a Water Scorpion is built almost exactly like a Giant Water Bug (p. 125), but on a much slimmer plan, and without swimming fringes on the legs. To look at a Water Scorpion, however, you'd think you were gazing at an underwater praying mantid (pp. 110–12). Water Scorpions do, indeed, catch their buggy prey with their forelegs, the way mantids do, but their forelegs are not spiked, and their heads do not turn to look at things all around them. As well, they have piercing, sucking mouthparts, not the chewing mouthparts of mantids. Amazingly, they can get up out of the water and fly to a new pond if the need arises—or at least the adults can. Young Water Scorpions look much like their parents, but without wings.

> **LENGTH:** up to 1.2 in, not including the breathing tube.
> **HABITAT:** ponds and lakes.

A Water Scorpion breathes through a siphon that extends out the back of its abdomen, which it uses like a snorkel. It is not a tube, but rather it is two parallel rods of cuticle with water-repellent hairs on them. Because of surface tension, water cannot penetrate past the hairs, so the siphon acts like a tube even though it does not form a solid barrier.

WHIRLIGIG BEETLES

Gyrinus spp.

The Whirligig Beetles are probably the coolest of all the water beetles. With the most efficient swimming legs in the entire animal world, they zip around on top of the water, spinning and whirling like super-fast bumper cars. If they need to, they can dive underwater and swim with the fishes, and they also have wings for when the time comes to find a new pond. Sometimes, dozens of them band together to form a frenetic flotilla on the surface.

If you have a microscope—and a whirligig specimen—you can see how amazing this bug's eyes are. Each eye is actually split in two! One half looks up into the air, and the other half watches down into the water. Of course, while the beetle is spinning and whirling at high speed, its eyes need all the help they can get, so the bug also uses its short, triangular antennae to "feel" their way through the twists and turns.

LENGTH: about 0.2 in.
HABITAT: ponds, lakes and streams.

Whirligig Beetles are predators, and they will eat any unfortunate bug they can catch on the water's surface. Even baby water striders (p. 124) are not fast enough to get away from them. And if another animal tries to eat a whirligig, it gets a mouthful of something that smells a lot like rotting fruit.

GIANT DIVING BEETLES

Dytiscus spp.

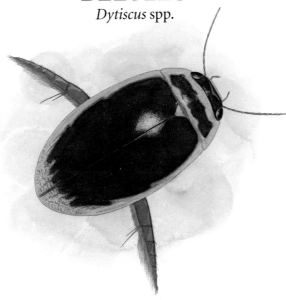

Next to the Giant Water Bugs (p. 125) and some really big Dragonfly larvae (p. 136), the Giant Diving Beetles are our biggest aquatic insects. They, too, are powerful predators that will eat almost anything they can overpower. If you keep pond critters in an aquarium, sooner or later you will find that there is only one left, and in most cases the survivor will be either a Giant Water Bug or a Giant Diving Beetle.

The most impressive member of this group of beetles is the Harris's Diving Beetle (*D. harrisii*), and a big one can be 1.6 inches long!

In most species of large diving beetles, the females can mature in either of two forms. The first form looks a lot like the male, with shiny black wing covers. The second form has grooves running the length of the wing covers, making it look at first glance like it must be a different species. A female with a white blob on the end of her abdomen has been mated—the white stuff discourages other males from mating with her again. Males have round sucker pads on their front feet for holding onto the slippery females. If

LENGTH: on average 1.1 in.
HABITAT: almost any freshwater, usually not flowing.

you notice a bad smell when handling these beetles, it is probably their defensive chemicals; they are powerful steroids, and predators respect them.

WATER SCAVENGER BEETLE

Hydrophilus triangularis

H ere we have a water beetle that is not a ferocious predator. Water scavengers are the gentle ones in the water beetle crowd (the adults, that is—the larvae are ferocious predators): they feed on plants and on various sorts of debris. *H. triangularis* is the biggest Water Scavenger Beetle in North America. Smaller types abound, mind you, and the large ones are certainly not typical of their family.

When Water Scavenger Beetles swim, they paddle like crazy with all six legs, but most of the time they cling to underwater plants. In many ways, they look like they are trying to pretend they are not underwater at all, like leaf beetles on the willows by the shore. Whereas diving beetles (p. 131) keep their air supply under their wings, hidden from view, a water scavenger keeps air both under its wings and all along its underside. Underwater, the beetle looks like it is coated with liquid mercury. To replenish the bubble, a water scavenger doesn't just bob to the surface either. Instead, it barely sticks its head up and then lets the air flow in around its antennae. For diving beetles, life is risky and fast; for water scavengers, it is careful and slow.

LENGTH: 1.4 in.
HABITAT: ponds and lakes.

SALMONFLY

Pteronarcys californica

The Salmonfly is also called the "Giant Stonefly," because it is our largest member of the stonefly group. Salmonflies are encountered frequently by people walking near rivers. When they least expect it there is suddenly a huge, flattened insect crawling on their clothes in a frenzied and highly unnerving manner. Of course, like most bugs, Salmonflies can't harm you, and they don't want to harm you. Still, most people would prefer to be introduced to stoneflies another way.

Another way that many people get to know this group is by reading dinosaur books. When you look at the paintings of the amphibians and reptiles that "ruled the earth" before the dinosaurs, the artist will often have added stoneflies, along with other ancient sorts of bugs, such as dragonflies and cockroaches. Leaving aside the fact that we all know that bugs have always ruled the earth, and that dinosaurs never did, it is interesting that stoneflies have remained more or less unchanged for about 300 million years. They are also interesting to watch in the here and now, especially when they drum their abdomens on

> **LENGTH:** 1.6 in or more, including the folded wings.
> **HABITAT:** common along rivers and streams.

the stems of plants as a courtship signal to the opposite sex. In flight, however, they are a far cry from masters of the air, proving that for almost one-third of a billion years, it really didn't matter.

MAYFLY LARVAE
Order Ephemeroptera

Some kinds of bugs seem to exist only for the sake of getting eaten by other creatures, which, of course, isn't true, although it sure seems that way. Mayflies and their larvae are one such group, and they are about as defenseless as a bug can get. The adults don't even feed.

The 100–200 species of Mayflies in this part of the world are either "crawlers," "burrowers" or "swimmers"—the one pictured here is a crawler. Each group has its own style of feeding, and they all eat such things as algae and detritus. Some species even sieve food from the water by using their hairy front feet. Depending on the species, Mayfly larvae can be found in streams, ponds, lakes or rivers. The easiest way to recognize a Mayfly larva is by the three prongs (feelers) at the tip of its abdomen and the fuzzy gills that line the sides of its abdomen.

When Mayflies emerge as adults, they generally live only a single day. Immediately before they reach adulthood, however, they go through an odd stage that no other insect goes through, during which they are called "duns" or "subimagos." Then they shed their skin again, wings and all, and become the short-lived true adults, which live only long enough to mate and lay eggs.

LENGTH: up to 1.2 in.
HABITAT: freshwater, mainly rivers and streams.

DAMSELFLY LARVAE
Order Odonata, Suborder Zygoptera

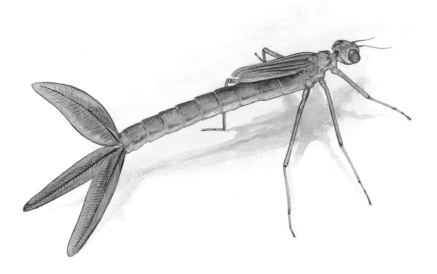

Here's an odd critter. At the back end of its long, slender body, you see what looks like three dead leaves. They are the insect's gills, with which it takes oxygen from the water. Six long legs help this bug to scramble among the underwater plants, where it watches for prey with its

LENGTH: up to 1.1 in.
HABITAT: ponds, lakes and streams.

bulging compound eyes. When a small, edible insect is spotted, the larva takes aim and—schnik!—the folded lower lip shoots out, many times the length of the larva's head, and grabs the unlucky prey like the tongue of a chameleon lizard.

Damselfly larvae are common in ponds and lakes, and they are easy to recognize. They are not good swimmers, mind you, and when they do have to swim, they wiggle through the water like people with their hands at their sides. If you look closely at the top of a Damselfly larva's thorax, you'll see four little wing pads. These pads will eventually become the wings of the adult Damselfly (pp. 116–18) when the larva finally climbs up out of the water and sheds its skin for the final time.

DRAGONFLY LARVAE

Order Odonata, Suborder Anisoptera

Damselfly larvae (p. 135) are weird, but Dragonfly larvae are even weirder. Both have the folding lower lip that catches prey, and both have big eyes and slender legs, but there the similarities seem to end. Dragonfly larvae are bigger, heavier and more powerful than Damselfly larvae. As well, instead of having leaf-like gills, they keep their gills inside the end of their abdomen, in their rectum. That means, I'm afraid, that they breathe with their butts. And when they need to swim, what do they do? They squirt water out their back ends and shoot through the pond with jet propulsion.

The larvae of the darner dragonflies (pp. 119–20) are long and streamlined, like the one shown here. Those of the skimmer dragonflies (pp. 121–23) have longer legs and fatter bodies, sometimes with lots of spikes out the sides.

LENGTH: up to 1.9 in.
HABITAT: ponds, lakes and streams.

Often, they become covered with algae and pond "guck." Perhaps the oddest Dragonfly larvae are the clubtails, which spend their lives partly buried in mud at the bottom of streams and rivers; they have smaller eyes and shorter legs than in the illustration. No matter what the species, Dragonfly larvae take at least a few months to grow up, and when they emerge to become adults, they crawl up on plants or on the sandy banks of rivers.

CADDISFLY LARVAE
Order Trichoptera

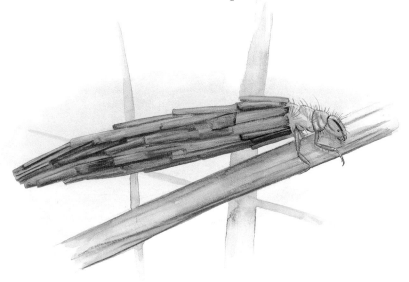

To most people, an adult Caddisfly doesn't quite qualify as a "cool" bug. These moth-like creatures are only moderately colorful, and the only obvious thing that sets them apart from other bugs is their long, wispy antennae. But every Caddisfly was once a larva, and Caddisfly larvae are just plain nifty. Most Caddisfly larvae are scavengers, but some eat algae, which they graze from rocks and water plants, and others are predators. While they are looking for food or eating it, they are constantly at risk from the underwater predators around them. So, these larvae protect themselves with cases—coverings for their soft, grub-like bodies. Some species make the cases out of twigs held together with silk and saliva, and others use pebbles, reeds or leaves. Most cases are straight, but some are coiled like a snail shell.

LENGTH: with case, up to 2.4 in.
HABITAT: ponds, lakes and streams.

To find Caddisfly larvae, look into a shallow pond and watch the bottom. Pretty soon, you'll see things move that you thought were just debris. These are the larval cases. Trout eat many of these insects, by the way, and experiments have shown that they recognize Caddisfly larvae by looking for their eyes. "If it has eyes, it must be alive," is the trout's rule, and when you think of it, that's not a bad way to find bugs yourself.

WATER TIGERS

Dytiscus spp.

Water Tiger is really just the larva of a Giant Diving Beetle (p. 131), and other sorts of diving beetles have similar larvae, too. The name "Water Tiger" leads some people to confuse the diving beetles and the tiger beetles (pp. 60–61), but tiger beetles live only on land and never in the water, at least in this part of the world.

A Water Tiger is a marvelous beast. It swims with all six legs, in a very graceful fashion, floating almost effortlessly through the pond. On its broad, flat head, a Water Tiger has simple eyes, not the large, compound eyes of the adults. As well, whereas the adults kill their prey by chewing on it with short but powerful jaws, the jaws of the Water Tiger are like two hypodermic needles. The Water Tiger swims up to its prey and then attacks quickly and savagely. Once a fish or tadpole has been impaled, digestive juices are injected and the prey dissolves inside its own body. You might think this would make the Water Tigers some of the most fearsome creatures in the pond, but they often fall prey to both Giant Water Bugs (p. 125) and the adults of their own species. Most Water Tigers prefer to eat small vertebrates, but some are more fond of eating insects instead. Like an adult diving beetle, a Water Tiger has to come to the surface to breathe, and its breathing hole is located right at the tip of its abdomen.

LENGTH: up to 2.8 in.
HABITAT: ponds and lakes.

SALMONFLY LARVA

Pteronarcys californica

At first glance, the larva of a Salmonfly (p. 133) might look a lot like a great big Mayfly larva (p. 134), but look closely and notice the differences. Salmonflies are a type of stonefly, and stoneflies form an insect order separate from the Mayflies. A stonefly larva has only two long feelers on the end of its abdomen, whereas a Mayfly larva usually has three. As an adult, a stonefly will still have two feelers; in fact, it will continue to look a whole lot like a larva, except with wings. When the biggest of our stoneflies emerge as adults, fishermen call them "Salmonflies," and trout go wild trying to eat as many as possible while the feast lasts.

LENGTH: up to 2 in.
HABITAT: rivers and streams.

Stoneflies don't live in ponds or lakes—they only like streams and rivers. Even then, they seem to prefer clear, fast-flowing water with lots of dissolved oxygen. Unlike Mayfly larvae, which have their gills on the sides of their abdomens, stonefly larva have their gills tucked into their "leg pits," so to speak. Without a powerful magnifying glass and an upside-down larva, they are tough to see.

What do stonefly larvae eat? Mostly water plants and algae, much like Caddisfly larvae (p. 137) and Water Scavenger Beetles (p. 132), but some are predators. With their powerful legs, they hold onto underwater rocks and fight the current that threatens to sweep them away.

SOW BUG

Oniscus asellus

I n general, insects are the bugs of the land, whereas crustaceans are the bugs of the sea. Some crustaceans, however, do live on land, although they need moist places in order to survive, because they breathe with modified gills. Remember, crabs are also crustaceans, and we have all seen the air-breathing hermit crabs that are such popular critters in pet stores. Even seashore crabs can spend a fair amount of time out of the water, up on rocks or sand.

The Sow Bug was accidentally introduced from—where else?—Europe. (Or at least this species was; there are also native ones.) It is interesting that European bugs generally do well when they are introduced to North America, but not the other way around. Sow Bugs are sometimes confused with Pill Bugs (*Armadillidium vulgare*—also a European import and sometimes incorrectly called "pill millipedes"), but Pill Bugs roll up into a ball when they are frightened, and Sow Bugs do not. They are both slow-moving, heavily armored creatures that are easily recognized by their many legs and their many-segmented shell of a body. Neither is harmful, and they both feed mostly on decaying material, both plant and animal. Because our gardens are almost completely unnatural ecosystems to begin with, the addition of Sow Bugs is not much different from adding another species of non-native flowering plant.

LENGTH: about 0.4 in.
HABITAT: gardens and disturbed areas.

GARDEN CENTIPEDES

Lithobius spp.

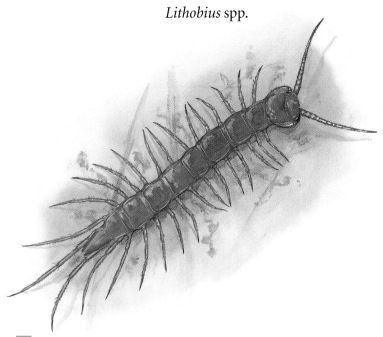

Lift a board or turn the soil in your average garden, and you're likely to find a centipede. The typical specimen is about 1 inch long and rusty orange in color. Centipedes move rapidly and twist like miniature snakes. They can squeeze into what seem like the tiniest openings in order to escape, which is probably why you also find them in basements so often. A poorly fitting window or a crack between wood and concrete will allow them to get in. Once in the house, however, a centipede is no longer in contact with its most cherished substance, moisture. Garden Centipedes quickly dry out indoors, and usually when you find them, they are desiccated and shriveled to about half their normal size.

LENGTH: up to about 1.2 in.
HABITAT: gardens and moist forests.

Centipedes are predators, and they have venomous fangs with which to subdue their prey. Our local species are not dangerous to people, but small children should still avoid handling them. If you can get a centipede to sit still for a moment, you'll see that each body segment carries one pair of legs, and the legs are set off to the sides. On a millipede (p. 142), each segment bears two pairs of legs, which are set underneath.

CLOWN MILLIPEDE

Harpaphe haydeniana

The main similarity between a millipede and a centipede is that both their names end in "-ipede," a word root that refers to their feet. Millipedes are slow-moving animals that feed on plants or detritus. Big millipedes, at least in this part of the world, are bigger than big centipedes. The Clown Millipede is noteworthy, because it produces cyanide as a defensive chemical. Some people call it the "Almond-scented Millipede"—the "almond" scent comes from the cyanide. The colors of this bug are a warning to would-be predators.

Millipedes have many more legs than centipedes, because they have twice as many pairs of legs per segment. With so many legs, there is a risk of them getting in each other's way. So a millipede moves its legs in slow, coordinated waves, starting at the back of its body and moving toward the head. Speaking of which, the antennae on a millipede's head give this creature a somewhat insect-like appearance from the neck forward, and indeed, the science of animal classification places millipedes closer to insects than to centipedes.

LENGTH: about 1.8 in.
HABITAT: forested areas with Douglas-fir.

For those readers who know that "millipede" means "1000 foot" and that "centipede" means "100 foot," please make a note that millipedes always have fewer than 1000 feet, and centipedes can have as few as 30. A 100-footed centipede is actually an impossibility, because centipedes always have an odd number of leg pairs. Therefore, a centipede might have $49 \times 2 = 98$ or $51 \times 2 = 102$ legs, but never an even 100.

SCORPIONS
Order Scorpionida

Scorpions are unmistakable, with their pincer claws, eight walking legs and long abdomen with a stinger at the end. One species that is found in Arizona and nearby areas, the Bark Scorpion (*Centruroides sculpturatus*), can be deadly venomous. The stings of our local species, how-

> **LENGTH:** usually about 1.4 in.
> **HABITAT:** dry, open areas.

ever, are apparently not much worse than a hornet's. Mind you, reports of the effect of our species' stings are few, and it's best not to take chances.

Even if you spend time in Scorpion habitat, you will probably have trouble finding any. By day, Scorpions stay under rocks. By night, they hunt on the ground for other small bugs, and then you can find them with a flashlight. If you have a portable fluorescent camping light, try putting a blacklight tube in it. Under the rays of ultraviolet light, Scorpions glow with an eerie green color, making them much easier to spot. This unusual property is apparently just an accident of nature, with no adaptive value to the Scorpion. After all, there is almost no UV radiation in the desert at night, so there is no way that this trait would ever show itself in nature. The people who see Scorpions glow green the most often are rockhounds looking for fluorescent minerals.

PSEUDOSCORPIONS

Order Pseudoscorpionida

The name "pseudoscorpion" means, literally, "false scorpion." Pseudoscorpions look like real Scorpions (p. 143) in miniature, except that they do not have stingers. In fact, their abdomens are blunt, much like those of spiders. Like Scorpions, they capture their prey with pincers, and in some species the pincers themselves (the pedipalps) have poison glands within them to help subdue smaller bugs. Most Pseudoscorpions live in leaf litter or decaying wood or under bark.

Like spiders, Pseudoscorpions produce silk (not from spinnerets on their abdomens, but from their jaws), which they use to form shelters in which they can pass the dangerous periods of overwintering and molting into a new skin. When a male is courting, he spins a silk mat and places a packet of sperm on it. The female picks up the sperm and uses it to fertilize her eggs. Like many arachnids, these females are good mothers. Most types keep their young in a brood pouch, where they are fed by a secretion from the mother's body. Because they rear relatively few young (a big brood contains 30), they are able to devote considerable attention to their babies, unlike most bugs, which produce hundreds or thousands of babies and then leave them to fend for themselves.

LENGTH: usually less than 0.2 in.
HABITAT: dry, open areas; under bark and in houses.

CAMEL SPIDERS

Family Eremobatidae

It would be unfair to characterize these arachnids as psychopathic killers, but hey, that's what they look like to most people who have encountered one. These oddball critters have an eerie combination of spiderish legs, a thin-walled bulbous abdomen, a bit of hairiness and a front end that is made up almost entirely of jaw-like pincers. These pincers are held in an up-and-down fashion, rather than side-to-side like most other bugs, and they make Camel Spiders look horrifically mammal-like when they chew. Their speckish eyes give no sense of intelligence whatsoever, and indeed Camel Spiders live mainly to kill other bugs.

> **LENGTH:** about 0.8 in.
> **HABITAT:** dry areas.

I suppose Camel Spiders also live to reproduce, and to their credit the mother guards her eggs for many weeks and stays with the young until they complete their first molt. Camel Spiders can be found in the same sorts of hot, dry habitats as scorpions. You will also see these arachnids called "wind-scorpions," "solpugids" and "sunspiders." However, I prefer "camel spider," the Arabian name, because we once had native camels in this part of the world, and these bugs watched the rise and fall of the North American camel, long before the arrival of civilization.

GARDEN HARVESTMEN
Order Opiliones

I used to call these creatures "daddy long-legs," and as a kid I thought they were spiders. I now try to use the more traditional name "harvestmen" to refer to them, because just about any long-legged bug gets called a daddy long-legs (crane flies especially). Harvestmen are not spiders. Spiders have two main body parts, but harvestmen have no constriction between the head and the abdomen. Harvestmen are also unable to produce silk. Their eyes are set in a little mound on the top of the body, and the eight legs extend out from the sides.

LENGTH: about 0.2 in, without the legs.
HABITAT: dark, moist places.

These critters are predatory, although, as you might imagine, they are no match for anything but small prey. They will also scavenge dead bugs or bits of decaying plants. Because harvestmen are such familiar garden bugs, various odd beliefs have developed about them. Some people believe that they are extremely venomous, even though it is tough to get them to bite. This belief is, as far as I can determine, complete baloney. Another weird story has to do with the belief that if your cow goes missing, you pull off a harvestman's leg and throw it on the ground, where it will point you in the right direction.

146

CALIFORNIA EBONY TARANTULA

Aphonopelma eutylenum

Thanks to their popularity as pets, tarantulas are no longer the misunderstood creatures they once were, but there are still many people who don't realize that they are not dangerously venomous. Tarantulas are our largest spiders, and most of the time when you see one it will be in the fall, and it will be a male wandering in search of a female. At other times of

> **LENGTH:** up to 1.8 in.
> **HABITAT:** open areas, chaparral and grasslands.

the year, both sexes are much more secretive, living in nooks and crannies, crevices and burrows. They are slow-growing, slow-moving creatures, and a healthy female can live for up to 35 years. When threatened, tarantulas tend not to bite, but to flick the hairs from the top of their abdomen with their legs. These hairs are barbed and cause itching, and they can be dangerous if you get them in your eyes.

Another related giant spider is the Calisoga Spider (*Calisoga longitarsus*). It is more gray in color than the California Ebony Tarantula, less hairy and much more aggressive.

147

JOHNSON'S JUMPER

Phidippus johnsoni

Even people with a deep-seated fear of spiders sometimes see a glimmer of cuteness in the members of the jumping spider family. Sure, they have eight legs and eight eyes, but they don't move in the same creepy way that other spiders do. Instead, they walk around in a more insect-like fashion (if you know what I mean), and they also jump. When you look at one up close, most of the time it will turn and look back with a pair of big bright eyes on the front of its head.

Jumping spiders have the best vision of any spider, and they can swivel their head around to examine whatever catches their interest. Add to these abilities the fact that some, like the Johnson's Jumper, have colorful bodies and iridescent fangs, and you have a spider with both a "face" and a personality. Many of the smaller jumping spider males also do complicated little courtship dances, waving their fangs, their palps (the little leggish things in front of the fangs) and their front legs like colored flags. If a female likes a male's dance, they will mate. These spiders are not aggressive, but the bite of the biggest ones (such as the Johnson's Jumper) can be painful and unsightly.

LENGTH: up to 0.4 in.
HABITAT: drier areas.

GOLDENROD FLOWER SPIDER

Misumena vatia

Here's the scenario: a big, fat spider waits patiently in a fresh blossom. Sometimes the spider is yellow, and sometimes it is white; sometimes these colors blend in perfectly with the flowers, and at other times they don't. An insect comes to the flower for a sip of nectar, and suddenly it becomes spider fodder.

My favorite story about this spider involved a butterfly, a Western Tailed Blue (*Everes amyntula*). The blue was flitting about in the greenery, stopping from time to time to sun itself, when it spied another blue. It flapped over to investigate, but the second butterfly seemed completely uninterested.

> **LENGTH:** females about 0.3 in; males about 0.1 in.
> **HABITAT:** meadows and clearings.

That's when I saw the female Goldenrod Flower Spider, tucked up between the purple flowers of the vetch they were all on. Before the first blue could comprehend the situation (if ever it could at all), the spider reached out, grabbed it and had two blues for lunch instead of one. Not only had the spider used the flower for an ambush, it had also used the first blue as a decoy!

Males of this species are smaller than the females, and they are darker in color. In a wild rose flower, the males look almost exactly like the pollen-bearing stamens—the best buggy camouflage I know of in this part of the world.

WESTERN BLACK WIDOW

Latrodectus hesperus

Black widows are easiest to find in drier areas, and they are not really common in the places where most people live. The best way to see one is to walk around in mid-summer and shine a flashlight down old mammal burrows, which are usually easy to find. The Western Black Widow spins a disorganized web, and it is just about the easiest spider in northern California to identify: it is shiny black and has a red hourglass on its tummy. The False Black Widows (*Steatoda* spp.) are more brownish and not as large.

The venom of these beasts can indeed be deadly, but fortunately they are shy and docile most of the time. Females do eat the males quite often after mating (thus the name "widow"), but this practice is actually fairly common among spiders, and it is not the macabre ritual that some people imagine. Apart from mammal burrows, old buildings and log piles, the best place to look for Western Black Widows (and related species) is in the grocery store, because many of them come in with fruits and vegetables. Some spiders may have red or orange markings on their backs, indicating they probably came from the southeastern states.

LENGTH: females to 0.5 in; males to 0.2 in.
HABITAT: dry areas.

YELLOW GARDEN SPIDER

Argiope aurantia

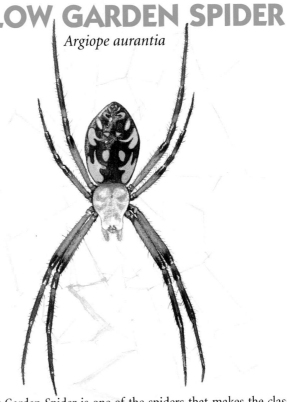

The Yellow Garden Spider is one of the spiders that makes the classic "orb" web that we all know and love: flat, with radiating spokes and a spiral of silk connecting them together. If you have never watched a spider make a web, you really owe it to yourself to do so. If nothing else, it is fascinating to think of how wondrous it is that any animal could do something so complex based on nothing but pre-programmed instinct. As one of the few animals with almost no innate behavior patterns (except perhaps things like smiling or yawning), we really can't imagine what it is like. The spider spins a perfect web every time, and it knows exactly how to get around on it, by holding the non-sticky threads, whereas the prey get caught in the sticky ones.

LENGTH: female, about 0.6 in.
HABITAT: gardens and shrubby places.

Tossing small insects into an orb-weaver's web is standard practice for outdoor kids, and we've all seen the spider wrap up its prey in silk and then deliver the death-fanging that injects the poison. It is all the more exciting to watch when the spider is a great big Yellow Garden Spider.

151

LONG-BODIED CELLAR SPIDER

Pholcus phalangioides

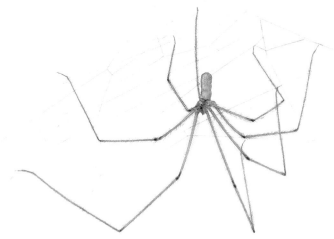

This bug is yet another one that commonly goes by the name "daddy long-legs," along with harvestmen, crane flies and who knows what else. I much prefer the name "Long-bodied Cellar Spider." These weird spiders seem to like the corners of household rooms, basements, attics and garages, as well as outside under the eaves. They must be incredibly patient, waiting for some other bug to wander into such an unlikely place and fall into their traps. The web of this species is roughly horizontal, but very messy, and sometimes it is more three-dimensional than two-dimensional. The Long-bodied Cellar Spider is also found in Europe, where the cellar was invented, I suppose. This spider has been with us in North America for so long that no one knows for sure if it is native here or not. Perhaps it stowed away in the holds of ships to get here.

LENGTH: body length, about 0.3 in; with legs, up to 2 in.
HABITAT: quiet places in buildings.

When you startle a Long-bodied Cellar Spider by turning on the light, it does something really neat. It starts swinging around in its web like a crazed gymnast, whirring back and forth so fast on the elastic web strands that you can't possibly follow it with your eyes. I wonder if it practices doing that in the dark when no one is looking?

BOOKS FOR BUGSTERS

Unlike with birds or mammals, there is no one book that covers the entire bug fauna of northern California—or of any county, state, province or country for that matter. You must be ready to face the fact that we have a great deal of knowledge about a few selected groups of bugs and almost no knowledge of all the others.

It is sad that many of the references that follow are out of print or hard to get hold of. Hopefully, we will soon see an improvement in the funding and support that "faunistic" studies receive. And let's hope that the work of detailing our arthropod fauna grows more and more vibrant in this new millennium, whether it is led by amateurs or professionals, or by people like me, on the border between the two.

The following books will take you a few steps further in your understanding of local bugs. I have avoided isolated papers in entomological journals, but if you are serious in your quest, these references will quickly lead you to them as well.

You might also try searching the worldwide web for information on specific sorts of bugs. As usual, some of it is well-researched and helpful, but most of it is not. Some groups, such as dragonflies, enjoy much better coverage on the web than others. It is better to search by scientific names, because there is a lot of variation in common names. If you do search for common names, be sure to try different possible forms, such as "twospot," "two-spot" and "two-spotted."

Books

Arnett, Ross H., Jr. 2000. *American Insects: A Handbook of the Insects of America North of Mexico.* Second Edition. CRC Press. Boca Raton, Fla.

Arnett, Ross H., Jr., N. M. Downie and H. E. Jaques. 1980. *How to Know the Beetles.* Second Edition. Wm. C. Brown Publishers. Dubuque, Iowa.

Bartlett Wright, Amy. 1993. *Peterson First Guide to Caterpillars of North America.* Houghton Mifflin Co., Boston.

Biggs, Kathy. 2000. *Common Dragonflies of California: A Beginner's Pocket Guide.* Azalea Creek Publishing, Sebastopol, California.

Chu, H.F., and Laurence K. Cutkomp. 1992. *How to Know the Immature Insects.* Pictured Key Nature Series. Wm. C. Brown Publishers. Dubuque, Iowa.

Furniss, R.L., and V.M. Carolin. 1977. *Western Forest Insects*. Miscellaneous Publication No. 1339. U.S. Department of Agriculture, Forest Service, Washington, D.C.

Garth, John S., and J.W. Tilden. 1986. *California Butterflies*. California Natural History Guides, No. 51. University of California Press. Berkeley.

Gordon, Robert D. 1985. "The Coccinellidae (Coleoptera) of America North of Mexico." *Journal of the New York Entomological Society,* Volume 93, No.1.

Hatch, Melvin H. 1953–1971. *The Beetles of the Pacific Northwest.* Volumes 1–5. University of Washington Press, Seattle.

Holland, W. J. 1968. *The Moth Book: A Popular Guide to a Knowledge of the Moths of North America*. Dover Publications Inc., New York.

Kaston, B. J. 1978. *How to Know the Spiders*. Pictured Key Nature Series. Wm. C. Brown Publishers, Dubuque, Iowa.

Needham, James G., Minter J. Westfall and Michael L. May. 2000. *Dragonflies of North America.* Scientific Publishers, Gainesville, Florida.

Opler, Paul A., and Amy Bartlett Wright. 1999. *A Field Guide to Western Butterflies*. Peterson Field Guide Series. Houghton Mifflin Co., Boston.

Otte, Daniel. 1981–1984. *The North American Grasshoppers.* Volume 1 and 2. Harvard University Press, Cambridge.

Powell, Jerry A., and Charles L. Hogue. 1979. *California Insects*. California Natural History Guides, No. 44. University of California Press, Berkeley.

Pyle, Robert Michael. 1981. *The Audubon Society Field Guide to North American Butterflies*. Alfred A. Knopf, New York.

———. 1992. *Handbook for Butterfly Watchers*. Houghton Mifflin Co., Boston.

Shaw, John. 1987. *John Shaw's Closeups in Nature: The Photographer's Guide to Techniques in the Field*. AMPHOTO, New York.

Stewart, Bob. 1997. *Common Butterflies of California*. West Coast Lady Press, Patagonia, Arizona.

Usinger, Robert L., ed. 1956. *Aquatic Insects of California, With Keys to the North American Genera and Californian Species*. University of California Press, Berkeley.

Westfall, Minter J., Jr., and Michael L. May. 1996. *Damselflies of North America*. Scientific Publishers, Gainesville, Florida.

White, Richard E. 1983. *A Field Guide to the Beetles of North America*. Peterson Field Guide Series. Houghton Mifflin Co., New York.

Organizations

Here is the contact information for various groups that can help you further your interest in bugs and enhance your enjoyment of the subject. Some organizations are local, and some are worldwide, but all have publications and meetings.

American Arachnological Society: c/o Norman I. Platnick, Membership Secretary. Department of Entomology, American Museum of Natural History, Central Park West at 79th Street, New York, NY 10024-5192.
website: http://americanarachnology.holycross.edu/
e-mail: <72737.3624@compuserve.com>

The Coleopterists' Society: contact the society's treasurer, currently Terry Seeno, CDFA-PPD, 3294 Meadowview Road, Sacramento, CA 95832-1448.
website: http://www.coleopsoc.org/
e-mail: <tseeno@ns.net>

Dragonfly Society of the Americas: c/o T. Donnelly, 2091 Partridge Lane, Binghamton, NY 13903.
website: http://www.afn.org/~iori/dsaintro.html
e-mail: <tdonnel@binghamton.edu>

Lepidopterists' Society: c/o Ernest H. Williams, Department of Biology, Hamilton College, Clinton, NY 13323.
website: http://www.furman.edu/~snyder/snyder/lep/
Membership applications c/o Julian P. Donahue, Natural History Museum of Los Angeles County, 900 Exposition Boulevard, Los Angeles, CA 90007-4057.
e-mail: <bugbooks@aol.com>

North American Butterfly Association: 4 Delaware Road, Morristown, NJ 07960.
website: http://www.naba.org/

Young Entomologists' Society: 1915 Peggy Place, Lansing, MI 48910-2553.
website: http://members.aol.com/yesbugs/bugclub.html
e-mail: <YESbugs@aol.com>

And finally, for entomological supplies and books, contact

Bio Quip Products Inc.: 17803 LaSalle Avenue, Gardena, CA, 90248-3602.
phone: (310) 324-0620, fax (310) 324-7931
e-mail: <bioquip@aol.com>

INDEX

Page numbers in **boldface** type refer to the primary, illustrated accounts.

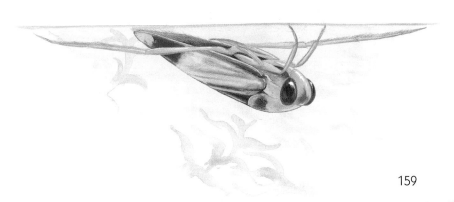

ABOUT THE AUTHOR

Since the age of five, John Acorn has been hopelessly fascinated by insects—a benign affliction that eventually led to a Master's degree in Entomology. His thesis work focused on tiger beetles, which are still among his favorite insects. Today, he works as an award-winning freelance writer, speaker and broadcaster, and he is best known as "Acorn, The Nature Nut," host of an international television series that appears on *Animal Planet*. John spends most of his spare time being exactly what you might expect—a bugster. He is also the author of Lone Pine's *Birds of the Pacific Northwest Coast* and *Bugs of Washington and Oregon*.

ABOUT THE ILLUSTRATOR

Ian Sheldon has been captivated by bugs since the age of three. Born in Canada, Ian later lived in South Africa, England and Singapore. Exposure to nature from so many different places enhanced his desire to study bugs and other creatures further, and he earned an award from the Zoological Society of London and a degree from Cambridge University. He has also completed a Master's degree in Ecotourism Development. Ian is an accomplished artist represented by galleries internationally, and he is both a writer and illustrator of many other nature guides, including Lone Pine's *Seashore of Northern and Central California* and *Animal Tracks of Northern California*.